Mental Liberation
in the Age of Thought Control

By Kerth Barker

Angelic Defenders & Demonic Abusers
Memoirs of a Satanic Ritual Abuse Survivor

Cannibalism, Blood Drinking
& High-Adept Satanism

Mental Liberation
in the Age of Thought Control
Deprogramming Satanic Ritual Abuse, MK Ultra,
Monarch & Illuminati Mind Control

Psychic Development
for Prosperity, Self Defense & Political Influence

See http://angelicdefenders.theshamecampaign.com

Mental Liberation
in the Age of Thought Control

Deprogramming Satanic Ritual Abuse, MK Ultra, Monarch & Illuminati Mind Control

Kerth Barker

Mental Liberation in the Age of Thought Control:
Deprogramming Satanic Ritual Abuse, MK Ultra,
Monarch & Illuminati Mind Control

All rights reserved
© Copyright 2014 Kerth R. Barker

Book design by Author Support Coop

Printed by Createspace, an Amazon.com company

It is advised that persons below the age of eighteen should avoid reading this book because of explicit descriptions of child abuse. If you have children in your home, please make sure that they do not have access to it.

Acknowledgements

I would like to thank these friends whose help made this book possible:
Rich Winkel ThoughtCrimeRadio.net
Jeanice Barcelo BirthOfANewEarth.com
Patricia Robinett TheShameCampaign.com

Contents

Introduction	1
Monarch Mind Control & The Culture of Celebrity	5
The Non-Glamorous Life of an MK-Ultra Sex Slave	7
The Use of Spirituality & "Truther" Materials for Deprogramming	15
Illuminati Brainwashing, Basic Principles	23
Kerth & Kathy	29
Trauma-Based Mind Control	35
The Illuminati	39
Emotional Trauma, Violence & Guilt	45
Exorcism & Catholicism	51
Toxic Therapy Systems	55
Fabian Technique	57
Fabian Lifestyle & Attitude	61
Exceptions to the Fabian Therapy Approach	65
A Brief History of Trauma-Based Mind Control	67
The Process of Trauma-Based Mind Control	69
A Visit to a Luciferian Temple	75
The Social Impact of Mind Control	79
Memory	81
Addressing Memory in Therapy	85
Command Words	89

The Process of Fabian Therapy	91
Journals	93
EMA – Episodic Memory Analysis	99
EMA Past Life Exploration	107
Extroversion Exercises	109
Semantical Deactivation Technique	115
A Typical Fabian Therapy Session	119
Advanced EMA Techniques	123
Basic Deprogramming Theory	127
Sexual Templates from Child Abuse	131
EMA to Reinforce Healthy Behavior	133
Concordance	137
Deactivating Mind Control Symbols	141
Other Uses of Fabian Therapy	143
Illuminati Cultural Mind Control	145
The Illuminati Power Structure	149
The Suppression of Fabian Therapy	151
Institutionalized & Medicalized Mind Control	155
Speaking Out	159
Fabian Therapy for Helping Abductees	161

A traditional Satanic Chant used to introduce certain types of meetings:

*You will now hear the story
of battles fierce and gory,
of all the pain and glory,
throughout Satanic History.*

*You will now hear of Demons,
from the Dark Nether Regions,
with all their plots and schemin',
throughout Satanic History.*

*Now hear the Cannon's Thunder,
as devil pirates plunder,
while all the Christians slumber,
throughout Satanic History...
throughout Satanic History.*

Introduction

When I was younger, I was subjected to Satanic Ritual Abuse. There were some people who helped me to get away from the cult. And there was a husband and wife team of therapists who helped to deprogram me and to heal me. I never knew their real names, but in this book I will call them *the Fabians*. They were members of the secret society known as the Illuminati, but they had come to reject its philosophy. They had been involved with some parts of the MK Ultra research project, but they also had become disillusioned with that experimental mind-control program. So they used what they knew of the human mind to create a therapeutic system for healing the victims of MK Ultra type mind control.

MK Ultra was the CIA's mind-control research for the behavior engineering of human beings. It officially began in 1953 and officially ended in 1973, but actually it continues on in secret. During the twenty-year period when it was called MK Ultra, it involved at least 80 institution and more than 180 researchers. The CIA hid its involvement behind front organizations. Universities, hospitals, prisons and pharmaceutical companies were involved. The research into mind control used mind-altering chemicals, hypnosis, sensory deprivation, isolation, psychological manipulation, sexual abuse and other forms of torture. Many illegal activities were engaged in. There was a great deal of variation in how the research was done by differing groups. Some groups were highly effective and drew little attention to themselves. However, some of the research groups were disastrous and left behind dozens of victims with ruined lives. When public awareness of the MK Ultra program became too great, the government pretended to close down the research in 1973. This mind control system continues on today with greater secrecy as *Project Monarch*.

When these Fabian therapists saw the damage that was caused by the trauma of MK Ultra, they felt bad about the part they had played in this research. So they secretly dedicated themselves to healing the victims of that type of mind control. These Fabian therapists were very politically connected, and they were well educated. They were considered to be geniuses in their field. They had access to advanced research that has never been publicly revealed. And they had a point of view about therapy and about human potential development which was largely unique. I think that their approach to understanding the mind is one that would be useful to anyone. I call their approach *Fabian Therapy*. This type of therapy avoids direct contact with painful memories. It's based on the idea that the human mind is an energy field which interacts with the brain and body. It's designed to allow the client to discharge the negative energy contained in painful memories through a cathartic process. It rehabilitates the memory system which has been damaged by trauma-containing memories. And it makes the client feel happier about life and more socially functional.

Unfortunately, the Fabian Therapy system was suppressed for political reasons. Without going into all the politics of this, I think you can understand that the CIA, who funded MK Ultra, might not have been happy about some of its former researchers coming up with methods for deprogramming MK Ultra victims. I didn't create this Fabian system, but I am one of the few people who understands how this system works, and I am the only one willing to talk about it publicly.

In recent years I've put out some internet articles on how Fabian Therapy works. And I've gotten some email responses back from people who are integrating ideas from what I've written about Fabian Therapy into their own healing process. These are survivors who are trying to recover from various types of mind control. Also I've had contact with therapists who are using Fabian Therapy techniques to help others.

One of the persons who have responded to my articles stands out for me. This woman had been in a cult that subjected her to the traumatic form of brainwashing called Monarch mind control. This created many problems for her. She had multiple personalities and periods of missing time.

After she disconnected from the cult she tried to use conventional talk therapy from a psychologist to help herself. This gave her moral support at a critical time, but she still couldn't remember things that had happened to her and she still experienced periods of missing time. She tried taking psychiatric drugs but those made her feel suicidal, so she stopped. She found a hypnotist and tried hypnotherapy. With his help, she was able to recover some memories and gain some control over her life, but she still had problems. Her hypnotist discovered some articles that I had been writing about Fabian Therapy, and he tried using some of the Fabian techniques that I'd described, and she improved greatly as a result. She felt happier and more stable. She gained a much needed control over her life. So although I'm not giving advice on how to do therapy with this book, I can say that some therapists and their clients have already found this information useful.

Different people come to mental liberation in different ways. And every person has to find his or her own path. But there can be tools which can help you in the process of achieving liberation. And that's what this book is about. *Mental Liberation in the Age of Thought Control* is a collection of stories, lessons and descriptions of techniques, all of which relate to deprogramming brainwashing and propaganda.

I want to make it clear that I'm not giving advice for mental health treatment. My only purpose here is to share information. What you choose to do with this information is your responsibility.

My hope is that some of this information might somehow be used to help the victims of harmful brainwashing techniques. However, it isn't just the victims of mind control and their therapists who will find this book useful. Anyone interested in psychology and the realization of human potential will find this information of interest. The more you understand how the human mind works, the more empowered you become. So this information isn't just about healing mind control; it's also about how you can increase your personal abilities.

This book reveals insider information as to how the Illuminati mind control methodology actually works. Some of this information may already be familiar to you, however this book also discusses the Fabian system for the healing and deprogramming of mind control. And this system has never been described by any other source. This book is a modest but unique revelation.

As well as this, I have known some persons who were the victims of various forms of Satanic Ritual mind control, and I am going to describe some of the things that were done to them. I think that it's important that the public knows the extent of depravity into which this mind-control system indulges.

This book may contain information that could be upsetting to anyone who has been subjected to traumatic mind control. Yet in reading this they may be able to better process their feelings about their abuse. My intention is that this book will give hope to those who seek recovery.

Whether they realize it or not, everybody in our present day culture has been subjected to thought-control technology. The experience of contemporary hospital birth is traumatic for many infants and mothers, and it has been designed to be that way. Circumcision is intentionally traumatic to infant boys. The educational system has been designed to be emotionally traumatic to the students. The *No Child Left Behind* and *Common Core State Standards* programs have been intentionally designed to be psychological torture for children. And there are many other ways that ordinary persons are traumatized by life. And much of this trauma is intentional. It has been engineered by those in power. The mass media propaganda and the entertainment business with its dark agenda are all part of a mind-control matrix. In a sense, the entire world culture has been subjected to Illuminati mind control. This book describes a path to mental liberation in this age of thought control. Therefore, this is a book for everyone.

MONARCH MIND CONTROL
& THE CULTURE OF CELEBRITY

The internet and tabloids are filled with stories about how celebrities are subjected to Monarch mind control. Whether it's true or not, certain celebrities have been promoted in the media as having been subjected to Monarch mind control – celebrities like Lady Gaga, Rihanna, Beyonce, Madonna, Angelina Jolie, Johnny Depp, Miley Cyrus, Katy Perry and others. The naive young people who look up to such entertainers are being sold on the idea that being in the Illuminati is hip. The idea of Illuminati mind control is sold to them as the path to wealth and fame. Monarch mind control is presented as being glamorous. But of course nothing could be further from the truth.

Consider the case of Katy Perry. I have no idea if she's actually been subjected to Monarch mind control, but her carefully crafted public image implies that she has been. And this implication is deliberate. She was raised in a Christian family, but now she's Lucifer's poster *"Gurl"*. Every video featuring her promotes the Illuminati's agenda and is filled with Satanic imagery. She produced a video called *Wide Awake* in which she hints that she's still a good Christian and has overcome her mind control. But the video is filled with Illuminati symbolism, and it ends with a Monarch butterfly flying over her, implying that she's still brainwashed. The videos and public performances that she's done since the release of *Wide Awake* all indicate that her celebrity status is still being used to promote the Illuminati's agenda.

And you should know that the phrase "wide awake" is a control command for waking up alter personalities. The *alter personality* is the personality that has been programmed into the mind control victim by the Illuminati brainwashers. So the *Wide Awake* video itself is being used to reinforce the programming of victims of Monarch mind control.

I don't wish to demonize Katy Perry. Most Christians are clueless about the nature of Satanism and many Christians work for wealthy Satanists without really fully understanding the true nature of their employers. And this may be the case for Katy Perry. I have no idea if Katy Perry even understands the Luciferian symbolism that is found throughout all of her videos. She may be the perfectly nice Christian that she says she is. She might not even understand the meaning of the Illuminati hand signals that she sometimes flashes. I think we should give her the benefit of any doubts we might have about her personal faith. But there is no doubt that she has made a "deal with the devil", as she has publicly admitted. The Illuminati manages her career, her videos and her performances. And they use her and the other celebrities to promote the idea that the life of a Monarch mind control slave is glamorous.

Monarch mind control is a system of brainwashing that was developed out of the MK Ultra mind-control research project funded through the CIA. After World War II, MK Ultra combined American intelligence on mind control with captured Nazi intelligence. As a child, I was subjected to some MK Ultra techniques, and I've known others who have been the victims of it. What I hope to convince you of is the fact that there is nothing glamorous about this type of mind control. And you should know that the persons who promote the use of mind control are among the most depraved individuals imaginable.

THE NON-GLAMOROUS LIFE OF
AN MK-ULTRA SEX SLAVE

The reality of mind control used to brainwash someone into sex work can be brutal. There is nothing glamorous about it. Tabloids and Hollywood movies may tease the public with the idea that mind-controlled sex workers are enjoying themselves. But the actuality of this phenomenon is tragic.

I could give you many examples of persons I've known whose lives were scarred by the mind control they were subjected to and the sex work they were forced to perform. But there is one MK Ultra mind-control victim that stands out. She was called *Daisy*. I only saw her up close and in person one time, and that was when I saw her ravaged corpse on the floor of a garage. She had committed suicide at the home of a wealthy Satanist, a man we called *the Baron*. Her corpse was dressed in a dirty rag of a dress, and her legs and arms had bruises and track marks from shooting up heroin. She looked completely ruined. I would learn of her life from photographs and stories told to me.

Originally her name was Veronica, but after she was subjected to MK Ultra mind control, her personality was completely erased, and she was programmed with a new personality named Daisy. All this was done under the authority of that powerful Satanic leader whose nickname was the Baron.

I never knew the Baron's real name. I was told that he had two homes. In one home he lived a normal life with his wife and children. He went to church on Sunday and was a respected member of his community. But he would be gone away on business for weeks at a time.

The Baron also owned a mansion of which his real family had no knowledge. In the basement of that mansion was a large black room containing a Satanic temple. He would conduct upscale orgies with his fellow Luciferians in the sex rooms located on the upper floors of this mansion. His staff were dedicated to him. He had many followers. He was called the Baron because he was like the robber barons of old. He was a ruthless businessman and he ran a criminal empire.

One day when he was driving down the road, he noticed Veronica walking along the street. He immediately felt lust for her. He got out of his car and quietly stalked her. He observed where she was headed. When she walked into a small eatery and sat at the counter, the Baron followed her in and sat next to her. They started up a conversation and there was a mutual attraction.

Veronica was a beautiful young woman. She was well educated. She had a good job and was independent. She was known for her intelligence and wit. Slowly, over a period of weeks and months, the Baron seduced her. Their relationship was very romantic. They took trips together to Europe and upscale resorts. He led Veronica to believe that he was unmarried. He revealed the fact that he was very wealthy. He hinted that someday he might marry her. He bought a small home for her by a lake near his mansion. Sometimes he would bring her to his mansion to show off how wealthy he was. But he never let her see the basement, the upstairs sex rooms, or his office.

I was only in his office one time. I knew that he always kept it locked. This was because his office was very revealing. The Baron was sexually perverse, and he had photos with sexual content plastered over all the walls of his office. He had a photo of himself standing nude in an English pond with his friend Aleister Crowley, the famous English occultist. This was an indication of the Baron's belief in sex magick, which is a type of psycho-sexual philosophy promoted by Crowley. The Baron was very proud of his own psycho-sexual obsessions. He had many photos of himself having sex with many different men and women of different ages. He had a photo of me dressed in women's lingerie when I was eleven years old kneeling before him performing fellatio while he sat in a throne-like chair dressed in a devil's outfit. This photo was in an elaborate frame that had a small light over it, illuminating the photo. And all of these photos were a reflection of the Baron's real personality. But his social persona was that of a dignified and Christian gentleman. He fanatically guarded his public persona and concealed his true nature. So he was very careful about who he let into his office.

But one day, back when he was still courting Veronica, he happened to leave his office door unlocked while she was visiting his home. Veronica knew nothing of the Baron's sexual perversity or his Satanism. She was only allowed to see his Christian gentlemanly persona. But all that changed in an instant.

The Baron had horses which he raised and sometimes sold. A mare was giving birth to the offspring of an expensive race horse, and the Baron wanted to observe the birth. After he left in a hurry, Veronica used this opportunity to sneak into the Baron's temporarily unlocked office. She knew that he was a man of many mysteries. She wanted to find out something about this wealthy man who she hoped would someday marry her. But it turned out that there were many things in his office which shocked her. The sexually explicit photos covering the walls were perhaps less offensive than the revelations that followed. On his desk the Baron kept photos of his wife and children which would have demonstrated to Veronica that the Baron had been misleading her all along. Apparently she also started going through his files and realized that he was a criminal and a Satanist. She must have felt betrayed as she realized the depth of his deception. Angry and upset, she took some of the incriminating photos and files with her as she ran away from the estate.

She knew a newspaper man who was an old friend of hers. She took these materials to this reporter and told him that she wanted him to write and publish an exposé on the Baron. Initially he agreed. But when this reporter took the photos and files to his newspaper's chief editor, he was yelled at and told that it was all a fraud. The editor took possession of all the files and photos. He told the reporter if he ever tried to write such a story he would be fired. What the reporter didn't know was that the editor was a Luciferian and the Baron's friend. The editor returned the files and photos to the Baron and told him what Veronica had tried to do.

The Baron was not only angry with her, he was also afraid of her. One rule that the Illuminati demands from its initiated members is invisibility. They must never allow themselves to be exposed, and they can never reveal what they know of the Illuminati. Every initiated member takes sacred oaths to this effect. The penalty for breaking the rule of invisibility is death. So the Baron had to take immediate action. He had his men abduct Veronica. They locked her up in a windowless room that was out in his barn.

The Baron had several persons working for him at that time who were experts on MK Ultra mind control, and so he made use of them. The first thing they did was to use some mind-control techniques on the reporter. Although he had been discouraged by his editor from writing an exposé on the Baron, this reporter, on his own, had started to research Satanism and the Illuminati. However, that night, when he was at his favorite bar, one of the Baron's men secretly put a drug into his drink. When he walked out of the bar in a drowsy state, he was whisked off to some place where the MK Ultra experts could work on him. Commands were implanted into his mind compelling him to forget about Veronica and to never write about Satanism. When the mind controllers were done with him, they parked his car in front of his home and left him asleep in the back seat. This reporter never realized that he had been the victim of mind control. The next day when he woke up on the back seat of his car, the reporter probably thought that he had gone on a bender the night before and had simply blacked out for a while. And it did turn out that this mind control was successful. This reporter never again investigated the Baron and he dropped all of his research into Satanism.

But what was done to Veronica was far more extreme.

First the Baron arranged so that it would appear that she had died. He made some bribes, and from a medical school or some such place he purchased a corpse that was the approximate height of Veronica. The Baron also knew a dental technician who could be bribed. The dental technician made up a dental chart for the corpse. The Baron's men broke into the office of Veronica's dentist. They filed the phony dental chart in her dentist's office under her name. Then the medical corpse was placed in Veronica's sports car. The car was set on fire and rolled down a hill. The body that was recovered was so badly burnt that it had to be identified with dental charts. In this way, Veronica was officially declared dead. Her family and friends buried the wrong corpse and mourned her death.

Secondly, the Baron didn't trust Veronica, so he had his MK Ultra experts completely erase her personality. They used an extreme form of sensory deprivation over a long period of time. She was so traumatized by this that her personality completely disassociated. Veronica never came back. Complete *tabula rasa* – a total blank slate. So this wasn't multiple personalities. This was personality erasure.

They renamed her Daisy, after the Baron's favorite mare, and began to reprogram her with a new personality. This was systematic *psychic driving*. At first she couldn't speak or eat on her own. She couldn't even use the toilet. They kept her in diapers and hand fed her. They talked baby talk to her. Eventually her ability to speak came back. After several weeks, she began to talk, walk and eat on her own. But she was like a child. And she had no memory of the past. She didn't know her name, what country she was in or anything about her past.

They began to train her to be the perfect sex slave. They had her look at TV shows and mimic the speech and behavior of sexy female characters. They showed her porno movies and had her mimic the behavior of the prostitutes starring in these films. Daisy became a shallow, obedient sex worker.

She was quite beautiful, and at first the Baron used her to make porno films with high production values to be sold to wealthy Luciferians in America and Europe. In these films she had sex with other young attractive men and women. With training she became something like a sexual athlete. She could perform any sex act in any position with multiple partners.

But a principle of mind control is that you never really erase the original personality with trauma-based mind control. The original core personality only becomes subconscious. So Veronica was still in there, although totally repressed and disconnected from the conscious mind. And this sex work went completely against her morals and personality. The more sex work she did, the more depressed she became. The only way they could motivate her to perform as a sex worker was to give her alcohol, so she became an alcoholic.

As her looks diminished, the Baron stopped using her in the high class porno films and started having her perform in films involving extreme deviant sex. One thing that fascinated the Baron was bestiality. He forced Daisy to have sex with horses, mules, sheep, dogs and goats. If she tried to refuse, the Baron would torture her until she obeyed. He especially liked having her filmed while she had sexual intercourse with goats.

In the Baron's office, I once saw a photo of him, Daisy and a horse. The horse was saddled and the Baron, naked, was standing up straight with his feet in the stirrups. He had a big smile on his face and an erection. In one hand he held a dog leash which went down to the dog collar around the neck of Daisy. She was naked and kneeling in a pile of manure next to the horse, which also had an erection. In the photo she was clearly seen to be sexually servicing the horse. Next to this photo was a different photo that had been taken shortly after the Baron had first met Veronica. In it, the two of them looked attractive and in love with each other. In that photo Veronica looked beautiful, intelligent and dignified. In his own twisted way, the Baron was proud of what he had done to this beautiful woman with whom he had once been in love. One thing that Satanists believe is that revenge is a religious duty. And the more insanely a Satanist pursues revenge, the more worldly power is given to him by Satan.

Over time, Daisy could only be motivated to perform degrading sex acts by being rewarded with heroin or cocaine. She became a heroin addict. And eventually her looks diminished to the point that she was of no value to the Baron as a sex worker. He set her up in a room in a poor part of town and sent her small amounts of money so she wouldn't starve. She became a cheap streetwalker so she could get enough money for alcohol and drugs. But eventually she was so beat up and ravaged that she couldn't even turn tricks for winos.

So she asked the Baron to send her more money. He refused. In response to this, she went to his estate and snuck in the back way. She found a rope and ladder. She hung herself to death on a tree in his backyard. This turned out to be most inconvenient for the Baron because he happened to be having a party at that time and everyone saw the corpse. But the Baron pretended that it was one of his famous practical jokes. And everyone at the party went along with this explanation whether they believed it or not. They were all Luciferians, so the Baron really had nothing to worry about. Nobody who really knew the Baron was likely to betray him. I happened to be one of the guests that night, so I saw the whole thing.

Daisy's corpse was cut down from the tree by the Baron's butlers. Her body was placed on the floor of his garage. He had his men dispose of her body elsewhere. They decided to try to have her body hung back up in another location with a suicide note which would not connect her to the Baron. In order to forge the suicide note they needed a sample of her handwriting. So the Baron had his butlers bring down some boxes containing memorabilia that he kept on Veronica and Daisy. In it he found a letter from Daisy. They put Daisy's corpse in the back of a van, and two of the Baron's men drove off with it.

The Baron left the garage and went back to his party. This left me alone in the garage with Bob, another man who worked for the Baron and whose story is told in my other books. Although I didn't know it at the time, Bob had become disillusioned with the Baron and with Satanism. I noticed some photos in the boxes. When I looked at them they shocked me. Bob began to tell me about Daisy and Veronica. Then he decided to take all the boxes that had been set out. We loaded them into the trunk of Bob's car. Then we went to say our goodbyes to the Baron.

We found him in the mansion and Bob thanked him for inviting us to the party. The Baron told us to come up to his office. This was the only time I was let in there. In a sense this was supposed to be an honor, because the Baron was very careful about who he let into his office. He made a big deal out of showing us the photo of me performing fellatio for his benefit while he was dressed as the devil. This was his way of telling me that he valued me as a possession. Looking at that photo of me in his office made me feel angry and ashamed, but out of fear I said nothing. It was also there in his office that I saw the two photos of Daisy and Veronica which I have described. I think the Baron was trying to make a point to us. He once had loved Veronica. But he felt that she had betrayed him. So he had avenged himself upon her in a way that was worse than if he had killed her. The once dignified and intelligent Veronica had been reduced to a cheap whore who entertained the Baron by performing acts of bestiality. Letting us see those photos was the Baron's way of warning us to never betray him. But, unbeknownst to the Baron, we had just stolen some of his boxes of Veronica memorabilia without his permission, and I wondered what Bob was up to, risking the wrath of a man who was insanely committed to revenge.

We said our goodbyes and left the party. Back at his house, Bob showed me some films and photos of Veronica/Daisy and told me the whole story. I had thought of Bob as being completely loyal to the Baron, but that night I began to realize that he wasn't.

I had been subjected to Satanic Ritual Abuse at various times throughout my childhood. I had been forced against my will to do sex work as a child. When I was with my mundane Christian family, I was Kerth. When I was with Luciferians, I was Kathy. I had two personalities, but they had become integrated over time. I have told this story in my book, *Angelic Defenders & Demonic Abusers*. Kathy was the name of my Luciferian sex worker personality. But the sex work I had done hadn't been anything like the intensely degrading experiences that Veronica/Daisy had been put through.

Sometimes young men from generational Satanist families are forced to do sex work during childhood as part of their training. The sex work tends to force them to emotionally bond with other Luciferians while at the same time giving them a sociopathic outlook on life. The sex work I did was as much for mind control purposes as anything else. The Baron had other child prostitutes he could have used instead of me. The sex work was a way of conditioning me. He wanted me to grow up to be a Satanist. The Baron had done sex work when he was a child. Many of the people in this world who you might think of as having great power were actually systematically abused as children. So in reality these powerful men are actually just brainwashed slaves themselves.

There was a great deal of pressure on me to join the Church of Satan. But after I learned what had been done to Veronica, I knew I had to resist the pressure to join the Church no matter what. I didn't want to become just another slave of Satan. So her death was not in vain. In spite of all her suffering, she helped to motivate me to do what I needed to do to escape Satanism.

Later on I heard the story of the two men whose job it was to dispose of Daisy's corpse. One of the men entrusted with this chore was called Ole Jack. Eventually he and I would become friends. He was a very unsympathetic person, but at times he could be righteous. He knew that Veronica had been horribly mistreated. However, although he understood the wrongness of what was done to her when she was alive, he never felt sympathy for the dead. He often told the story of that night when they tried to dispose of Daisy's corpse. Apparently everything imaginable had gone wrong. It was described to me as a comedy of errors. Finally, because of circumstances, they wound up burying her corpse in an unmarked grave in a garbage dump. So much for the glamorous life of an MK Ultra mind-control sex worker.

The Use of Spirituality & "Truther" Materials for Deprogramming

The entertainment industry has hinted at the idea that Monarch mind control somehow is glamorous and that it may even give its recipients enhanced abilities. But the reality is that the Illuminati is run by deceptive and decadent aristocrats. Once you accept the fact that Monarch mind control is not a system of therapy or of self-improvement and that it is a degrading process, then you can appreciate the need to heal and deprogram the victims of this type of brainwashing.

I have been in communication with some survivors of Monarch mind control and the therapists who try to help them. These are people who have been subjected to Monarch mind control and who are attempting to recover from its effects. I myself am a survivor of Satanic Ritual Abuse and some MK Ultra techniques. What I know of Monarch mind control is that it's based on MK Ultra research and that it is a very precise technology. The programing of Monarch is based not just on spoken language but also on the projection of images into the mind. Drugs and suggestions are used in a very exacting way. It's a sophisticated process. Treatment for recover from this can take a great deal of time and can be very difficult. I have been involved with survivors of mind control abuse at various times in my life and in various ways. However, in recent months, my only contact with such survivors has been through emails and letters. Over the last few years I have put some articles on the internet describing some recovery methods for mind control. So some people interested in these methods have communicated with me. And some of these discussions have also gone into related subjects.

One thing that many deprogrammers have found useful is to approach this subject of deprogramming on an intellectual level. There are a number of well known "Truthers" such as Ellen Hodgson Brown, Alex Jones, David Icke and others. They have talked about how this global system of corruption operates. This type of analysis is called *Deep Politics*. This is where a researcher goes into the root causes of what's going on, rather than getting hung up on the superficiality of partisan politics. Materials on deep politics and truther issues, such as *9/11 Truth*, can awaken a brainwashed person, at least on an intellectual level. Rather than going directly into their personal experience of abuse, they intellectually comprehend how the entire world culture has been abused. So this can be the first step in a process of mental liberation.

Some people wrongly assume that Christianity is the cure for Satanic Ritual Abuse. I'm a Christian, and I've found this faith useful to me. I have personally found that simple Christian prayer is very important to my recovery and ongoing well-being. Heart-centered and loving prayer can be very powerful. But I have to acknowledge that some Christian Churches are themselves founded on a type of mind control. And the use of mind control in other religions is common. In fact, the CIA deliberately created mind-control cults in the US during the 1950s and 1960s, and some of those cults were religions. To exchange the mind-control system of Satanism for some other type of religious mind control is not an improvement. For a person who has been subjected to Satanic Ritual Abuse to enter into another system of mental abuse can create problems for that person. Some Christian ministers are very narrow-minded, invalidating and judgmental. If you are drawn to the spiritual path of Christianity, you need to find a fellowship that is open-minded, life-affirming and heart-centered. So you have to be very careful if you are seeking to liberate yourself from mind control or if you are trying to help somebody else. You need to find an approach to mental liberation which does only good and doesn't do more harm.

This book that you are now reading – *Mental Liberation in the Age of Thought Control* – contains in it what I know of the process for deprograming MK Ultra and Satanic Ritual Abuse. I gained this information as a survivor who escaped a Satanic cult, and as someone who has worked therapeutically with other survivors at various times in my life. Also, over the years I've received some insider information about Monarch mind control. So I've included these insights in this book. The information contained in this book is the same information that I have been privately sharing with recovering survivors and the therapists who are working with them.

The problem with some of the techniques that I've taught, and with methods which other deprogrammers have developed, is that they work slowly over a long period of time. In some cases this takes years of difficult work. So we always look for something that can accelerate the process.

One thing that I've found personally helpful is the Reiki holistic healing practice. I am myself a Reiki master. Let me explain about Reiki just in case you are unfamiliar with it. The word *Reiki* translates from Japanese to mean *Universal Life Force*. *Rei* means *universal* and *ki* means *life force*. It's pronounced "ray key". Reiki is a field of invisible energy which permeates the entire Cosmos. It does only good and brings all living things into health and harmony. You could say that Reiki only operates at the higher vibrational level of unconditional love. A Reiki healer accepts this Universal Life Force through the crown of the head and projects it outward through the palms of the hands. This may be a hands-on healing practice, or it may be done remotely, at a distance. This is done to heal someone spiritually, mentally and physically. It's a subtle but tangible healing practice.

> *Then they began laying their hands on them,*
> *and they were receiving the Holy Spirit.* – Acts 8:17

Some Reiki healers are Christians who think of Reiki as a Christian practice. The Japanese word *rei* can also be translated as *divine* or *holy*, and the word *ki* can be translated as *spirit*. So Reiki could be thought of as a word for the Holy Spirit. Reiki was developed in the 1920s by a Japanese Buddhist named Mikao Usui. However some of the early practitioners and promoters of Reiki practice were Japanese Christians. Some have tried to define Reiki practice as a Christo-Buddhist practice. However I think that Reiki healing practice it most accurately thought of as a non-religious spiritual practice which promotes holistic health.

The way that Mikao Usui came into his healing practice is this: he had gone on a pilgrimage to Mt. Kurama in Japan, a home to temples, shrines and sacred traditions. During a period of fasting and prayer, Mikao Usui had what some might call a "shamanic" experience. During this experience a powerful flow of spiritual energy came into the crown of his head. Apparently he had visions and saw certain sacred symbols. After this he found that he could heal people with Reiki energy which he projected from his palms. Some call this practice *palm healing*.

Eventually Mikao Usui began to teach this practice to others. They in turn taught others, and so forth. Through a succession of teachers, every

Reiki palm healer inherits this ability. So every Reiki palm healer, myself included, is personally connected to Mikao Usui and the experience he had on Mt. Kurama.

As a Christian, I feel no conflict with my Reiki practice and Christianity. However my personal relationship with Jesus Christ and Mary the Mother of Christ still represents, for me, my most important source of spirituality. Whatever your religious or non-religious philosophy, it's very important to find a spiritual practice which centers you in heartfelt goodwill for humanity and all life.

Also there is the study of *truther* books and videos. These would be well-researched books which challenge the lies and propaganda put out by the corporate-owned mass media. David Icke's *Perception Deception* would be an example of a truther book. Alex Jones sells truther books on his website. Some therapists who treat victims of Monarch mind control have used truther materials as a tool for deprogramming. One technique is that a therapist will show a truther video to a mind-control victim, and then watch the recovering victim as he or she watches the video. If the recovering victim shows signs of confusion or anxiety, the therapist stops the video and talks with his or her client. This allows the opportunity for explanations or the processing of negative emotions.

When it comes to written materials, some recovering victims have studied them in a very specific and intensive way. In recent years I've worked with a group of psychics who oppose the Illuminati. They've taught me a reading technique that I've taught to others. This technique is called *scan-subvocalize-cognize*. This reading technique subtlety evokes psychic power in the act of study to enhance comprehension. In a sense this is really a spiritual practice.

Scan-subvocalize-cognize is a reading technique that encourages a higher level of comprehension. It works like this:

Scan

You *scan* a section of written material quickly by moving your finger or a pointer across each line starting from the beginning and moving sequentially to the end. This is not speed reading because you aren't trying to actually read the text at this point. You are simply scanning line after line in the text, searching for words that you might wish to look up in a dictionary. This is an intuitive action. In a sense it doesn't even matter why you might want to look up a particular word. Maybe the word is unfamiliar, maybe you just feel like looking up that particular word in a dictionary.

The real reason for scanning for words to look up in the dictionary is to give your conscious/analytical mind something to do while you perform the physical action of scanning. Most people think of psychic ability as being a purely mental activity. But I have known some very powerful psychics, and they all believe that psychic ability is a mind-body practice that involves physical behavior and a physical sensitivity. That is to say, you evoke the projection of your psychic powers with your physical actions and you receive psychic insights with a sensitivity to feelings in your physical body. So psychic ability is a physical discipline which results in a mental or emotional realization. This is because psychic powers arise through the subconscious mind from the superconscious psychic mind. The subconscious mind has a neurological/mental barrier between it and the conscious mind. Some call this barrier the limen. The limen is the threshold that defines the limits of the analytical conscious mind as well as the limits of the intuitive subconscious mind. The conscious mind is associated with the logic and language activities of the brain's left hemisphere. The subconscious mind is associated with the intuitive and imaginative activities of the brain's right hemisphere. What separates the left and right hemispheres is what might be called a lack of wiring in the brain. What connects the conscious mind and the subconscious mind together is the nervous system of the physical body. So all valid psychic practices involve physical actions and a sensitivity to physical feelings.

And that's what this scanning practice is. You physically move the pointer or your finger along the lines of the text while at the same time moving your eyes along with the pointer. You should do this is a slow, even manner. You don't even try to comprehend the written text at this point. You are really just hunting for those words which feel unfamiliar. These would be words whose meanings are uncertain to you. While you are scanning like this, you will sometimes find that you have a feeling of discomfort in your body. You may yawn, you may feel drowsy, you may suddenly feel bored, you may suddenly feel angry for no reason or it may just be a feeling of something being wrong. When you have such a feeling, look back at the text you've just scanned and see if any word pops out at you. When you notice such a word, that feels like you should look it up, write it down on a list. After you have scanned the section of text, you then look up all those words in a dictionary and see how they apply to the text. But if you don't feel that you need to look up any words, that's fine also. This is because the physical act of scanning opens up the subconscious mind to a deep psychic decoding of the meaning of the text.

In his book *Perception Deception*, David Icke says, "The universe is a tapestry of resonating waveform information fields... from which we decode information and to which we also 'post' information... I call this waveform construct the *Metaphysical Universe* or the *Cosmic Internet*."

What David Icke is referring to as the Metaphysical Universe is what some advanced psychics would call the Universal Mind. Some Remote Viewers call this the Great Unknown. Edgar Cayce once said that the subconscious mind is the doorway to the superconscious mind which is the source of your psychic powers. Whatever you choose to call this Metaphysical Universe, all information already exists there, and anything that is coded into written language is only a partial reflection of this universal knowledge. So with the combination of your analytical mind with your psychic powers you can both comprehend and transcend the knowledge in a written text.

So the scanning process is a step toward intensively decoding information that is represented by written words. First you intuitively sense the information before you analytically think about it. And that's all you're doing with the scanning process; you're intuitively getting a feeling for the material.

Another thing which connects the left and right hemispheres, and thus the conscious and subconscious minds, is the visual cortex. When you close your eyes, you invite imagination into your consciousness. The sleep dreams that you remember when you wake up are visual-based because they are messages from your subconscious mind to your conscious mind. When your eyes are open, and you are engaged in visual activity, you are evoking the powers of your subconscious mind, and that in turn brings into play your superconscious psychic powers. So as strange as this may seem to you, when you quickly glance at the words, without trying to read them in a traditional sense, that actually invites psychic ability into your reading process. You have to experience this to understand it.

Subvocalize

The next step in this decoding process is *subvocalization*. Again this is a physical process. Subvocalization is the process of reading a text out loud in a barely audible whispered voice. The psychics I've worked with have done a great deal of scientific research, and they've told me that when a person is scanning, a different part of the brain is activated than when a person is subvocalizing.

Again you want to give the conscious/analytical mind a chore to do to keep it busy while you perform the subvocalization process. So while you subvocalize the section of the text, hunt for words to look up in a dictionary. During the subvocalization process you quietly read the words out loud in a slow, even, whispered voice. While subvocalizing you might notice that your voice falters or that you mispronounce a word. You might feel the urge to cough suddenly or you may have some similar physical response. When you feel this, check back in the text you have just read and look for any words that pop up into your attention. When you find such words, write them down in a list. When you've finished subvocalizing the section, look up those words in a dictionary and check what their meanings would be in the context of the the written text. If you don't come across any words to look up, again that is OK. This is because the process of subvocalization is another step in the process of deeply decoding information.

During the subvocalization process, don't try to fully comprehend what you are reading. It's enough to just begin to have a feeling what what the author is conveying. Don't really think about what you are reading as you subvocalize, just go through the physical process of subvocalization and pay attention to what you what you physically feel.

Cognize

Once you've scanned and subvocalized, as well as looked up words in a dictionary (when necessary), then you actually read the text as you would normally do. To *cognize* is to understand or know something. Scanning and subvocalization are physical/psychic processes. When you finally cognize the text, the reading of it is a mental process rather than a physical/psychic discipline. So you are not really physically involving yourself so much in this final reading. Your full attention is on understanding the text. But by preceding the final reading of the text with the physical/psychic processes of scanning and subvocalizing, you have prepared your conscious mind to cognize this information deeply.

It's best to apply the scan-subvocalize-cognize reading method to sections of an overall text which are only a few pages long. You scan a few pages, then you subvocalize those pages and then you finally read those pages for comprehension.

I've heard various theories as to why scan-subvocalize-cognize works. The group of researchers who developed this technique were highly educated. One theory is that scan-subvocalize-cognize balances the activities of the intuitive right hemisphere of the brain with the analytical left hemisphere of the brain. Most reading of a text is a purely left-brain activity, so people become bogged down when they read too much. Apparently the brain is designed to balance left and right brain activities. And that's what scan-subvocalize-cognize does.

I don't know for certain why it works, but I do know that it does work. It's worked for other people to whom I've taught this process, and it's worked for me. Anybody who knows me knows that I don't get along well with computers and other machines. But we all need to use these devices, so it's necessary to study technical materials. When I do need to read a technical paper, I always use scan-subvocalize-cognize, and this technique makes it possible for me to comprehend those subjects which were once incomprehensible to me.

If you are trying to figure out what truther materials to use in the deprogramming of yourself or others, consider the works of Ellen Hodgson Brown, Alex Jones, David Icke as well as the websites that I've listed above.

Illuminati Brainwashing, Basic Principles

There is a basic theory for Illuminati mind control. There are four basic concepts involved in all its mind control methods. These concepts can be applied in different ways, and they can be used with different levels of intensity. Outside the Illuminati these terms are sometimes intentionally defined differently to conceal this information from the general public. So I'm describing these concepts here as the Illuminati mind controllers would understand them. They are *depatterning, tabula rasa, psychic driving* and *disassociation*.

Depatterning

Depatterning is the act of changing someone's pattern of thinking. This may be a temporary phenomena or a permanent one. Depatterning can be used for creative purposes or for harmful ones. Forms of depatterning can be very harsh and cruel, such as shock treatment. But there are other applications of this concept. For example, the singing that goes on in a church tends to put people into a slight state of relaxation which makes them open to the sermon that will follow. So the ordinary pattern of secular thought that goes on outside of Church is depatterned by the hymns and spiritual music being performed. I'm not saying that Christian hymns are a form of Illuminati mind control. I'm just pointing out that the concept of depatterning has many applications, not just in brainwashing.

Another example of depatterning can have to do with wearing clothing different from what is normally worn. The clothing you wear defines your role in society. A soldier going to war wears a military uniform – depatterning his civilian way of thinking. If a gay man, who normally dresses and acts masculine, puts on a drag costume at a gay bar, he's depatterning his normal way of thought and behavior to give himself permission to behave in an overtly sexual way.

Depatterning is not necessarily mind control, it's just something that is done to allow a different pattern of thinking and behavior to emerge. If it's done consciously and rationally, depatterning can be an expression of individual free will. It would be any practice or ritual that allows you to shift the pattern of your thoughts and behavior.

There is an interesting story that is often told about the Satanist Aleister Crowley. One night, he demonstrated depatterning to a friend. He walked behind a stranger on the street, exactly mimicking the stranger's footsteps so that the sound of his own footsteps would be subliminally entrained into the mind of the stranger. (*Entrainment* is when you establish a pattern into a person's mind through rhythm and repetition.) Once Crowley had subliminally entrained the stranger's pattern of walking through the sound of his own footsteps, he deliberately made a series of loud missteps. This caused the stranger in front of him to instantly stumble without understanding why.

However, brainwashing takes depatterning to an extreme as a way of attacking the personality of the victim. Here depatterning is used as a form of abuse. This might come about as any activity that overwhelms and disorients the individual. This turns off the reasoning mind and opens the subconscious mind to programming. And always such programming goes against the welfare and free will of the individual.

One common approach to depatterning is to shame a person through the confession of sins or mistakes. There are many common systems of indoctrination which start out with this process. I'm not saying that the Illuminati are the only ones who use mind control. They are just the most extreme. Actually the entire culture of our world is obsessed with mind control, and many forms of organized religion use it. Through the confession of sins, the person is beaten down emotionally through a process of self-invalidation. Depatterning is the deconstruction of the ego by systematically attacking the self-esteem of the individual. Of course people do make mistakes in life, and it's important to recognize mistakes so that change can take place, but to begin a therapy process by having the subjects list their mistakes or sins is an attack upon the ego. Individuals need strong, healthy egos. This type of sin confessing is a way to manipulate people with guilt. It depatterns the person's normal self-esteem.

When depatterning is taken to an extreme, it invalidates and erases the individual's natural core personality.

Tabula rasa

Tabula rasa is from Latin. It literally means tablet erasure or an erased tablet. This is where the mind of the individual is turned into a blank slate. It's the complete or partial erasure of the individual's personality. This is the goal of the mind controllers.

Tabula rasa can be done on the level of an individual or of a culture. When tyrants burn books, they are erasing the cultural memory of a people. They want to turn the culture into a blank slate so they can program the people with a new culture.

The New World Order that the globalists are trying to promote is based on the concept of tabula rasa. They want to erase all existing governments in order to create a new, all powerful, global government. They want to erase all religions, languages, currencies and cultures. Then they will be able to impose a single new religion, language, currency and culture upon all of their slaves.

Psychic driving

The psyche is the mind of the individual. *Psychic driving* is the motivations which are programmed into people's minds to compel their behaviors. Once the mind controller has achieved tabula rasa in the mind of the victim, psychic driving is the writing of a new program onto that blank slate. Psychic driving is the creation of a new personality once the brainwasher has achieved the erasure of the old personality.

Psychic driving can take place on the level of a single individual or on the level of an entire culture. The mass media in modern America is very involved in the psychic driving of the entire culture.

Psychic driving can take many different forms. One unsuccessful method was experimented with by the Canadian MK Ultra researcher Donald Ewen Cameron. His form of psychic driving was to put people on LSD and make them listen to tape-recorded messages over and over again. Those tape-recorded messages failed to shape or influence the victims' behavior in any way, but this process did drive the victims completely insane and ruined their lives.

I don't want to describe the psychic driving methods which do work, because I don't want to teach people how to brainwash. I'm only interested in teaching how to deprogram and heal the mind. To do that, it's enough to understand the basic concept of psychic driving.

And I want to point out also that the ultimate form of psychic driving is actually done through psychic abilities. This is also sometimes referred to as *remote influencing*, and it is a very precise technology. This type of psychic driving can be done to a single individual, but powerful psychic adepts can also do it on a cultural level involving the minds of untold numbers of people. For example, when the 9/11 false flag operation was being executed, Satanists performed occult rituals to psychically influence the minds of hundreds of millions of U.S. citizens.

Dissociation

Dissociation is the detachment of the mind from emotions and physical feelings. Dissociation is essential to the process of mind control. People express their individual will power because of their emotions and physical feelings. You are free to the extent that you can feel and act upon what you feel. Those who lose their ability to connect with their authentic emotions and physical feelings have lost their freedom.

A brainwashed sex slave will feel ashamed of being forced to perform deviant sex acts, but that feeling of shame is detached from the mental processes that control speech and behavior. So the sex slave will talk and behave as if she is enjoying a sex act which she actually finds repulsive. She will pretend to feel pleasure during a sex act which is actually painful.

Dissociation is the disconnection of the individual's willpower so that the will of a controller can override it. When someone is completely dissociated, a new personality will emerge. This new personality is a projection of the desires or intentions of the programmer. Dissociation is achieved with physical and/or emotional torture, and this is the basis of the multiple personality phenomena.

The cult of celebrity is promoted as a way of encouraging this type of mind control. Hollywood actors and music entertainers make it seem glamorous to originate different characters. Celebrities dramatize multiple characters in their entertainment acts. Hollywood and music industry leaders secretly intend this as a dramatization of multiple personality syndrome. Pretending to be different persons and having different looks might seem like harmless fun – and I'm sure that it is sometimes – but the worship of these celebrities is actually a form of social mind control. The public is being taught that it's empowering to have many different personalities. The public is being convinced that genuine authenticity is boring and mundane. But the truth is that centering yourself in your authentic personality is your greatest point of power.

Kerth & Kathy

I wasn't subjected to the ultra-extreme type of torture that was used to erase the personality of Veronica. But I was subjected to some MK Ultra techniques, as well as some traditional techniques of Satanic Ritual Abuse, so I did develop two distinct personalities. These were Kerth and Kathy.

Kerth lived with his mundane Christian family and was an ordinary little boy. Kathy dressed in girl's clothing, witnessed Satanic rituals, socialized with adult members of Luciferian secret societies, and was sometimes coerced into doing sex work – usually with adult men.

Most of the sex work I did as a child basically consisted of some sexual role-playing to help get the client's penis hard, then I would put a condom on his erection and perform a method of fellatio. The idea was to lick the head of the penis in the same fashion as I might lick an ice cream cone. A lubricant would be used on the shaft of his penis and I would stroke the shaft of the penis with my hands until it ejaculated. If the penis was uncircumcised, this chore tended to be easier. It was more difficult to use this technique effectively with a circumcised penis. And often it was more difficult to bring a circumcised penis to erection. While I was performing fellatio, two or more other sex workers would be massaging the man's body. The idea was to overwhelm him with pleasure so that he wouldn't try to take control of the session.

For one thing, some of the sex work I did was for the purpose of blackmail. And the hidden movie cameras that were used to secretly film the sex act were in fixed positions on the other side of a two-way mirror. So the sex workers had to direct the man onto a bed or chair that was in the focus of the camera. It was necessary for the purposes of blackmail that the man's face be clearly seen in the film and the fact that he was having sex with a male child had to be clear as well. If he tried to take control of the session, he might wander outside the focus of the camera. Also there was the threat that the client might anally rape me which was incredibly painful, especially if he had a large penis. As a child, I personally felt threatened by men's penises. I tended to think of them as potential objects of torture. But if the penis was managed appropriately with fellatio then the man would have an orgasm before his erect penis could be turned into a weapon. Some of the more skilled sex workers tried to prolong the pleasure of sex by delaying the orgasm while sustaining the erection. The other sex workers I knew considered this to be the art of fellatio. If the man was a regular client, I had to concentrate on the art of fellatio. But if the sex work was just for blackmail, I didn't care about that. In such cases I wanted the penis to ejaculate as soon as possible so I could run out of the room before the subject recovered. That way I could avoid further molestation. After all, the whole point of this chore was to acquire a blackmail film for the Baron.

The Baron might use the film to acquire blackmail money from a man, but that was rare. The real objective was to obligate the man to do something which the Baron wanted done. This might be corporate espionage, insider information on stock market trends or some type of political intrigue. Also this was a way to compel a man to become entangled with Satanic secret societies. If the Baron wanted to ask a man to join his secret society, he needed to have something he could use to blackmail him. That way the man wouldn't have the option of going public with the knowledge of the secret society once he was asked to join it. So the ability to blackmail men in this way was essential to the Baron's work.

The person who managed my sex work, my pimp, was the man we called Bob, the man who worked for the Baron. The way that Bob trained me, and the basic technique of sex work that we used to make blackmail films, was not some random process. The CIA had done a classified study on how to train children to be pedophiliac sex workers, and how to use their sex work for blackmail purposes. This study had involved sexologists, doctors and psychiatrists. They had concluded that the fellatio technique described above did the least physical damage to the child. And the child could service more clients if he or she used that method. The study described methods for training children, in the most efficient manner, to become sex workers. Bob had a copy of a book that contained this CIA report. And one day, when I had grown to be a teenager, I found a copy of this book by chance and read it. The practice of using children for sex work to create blackmail movies isn't some rare phenomena. The practice of highly organized child sex rings is woven into the institutions of government and finance around the world. The science and a technology of pedophilia was created by the CIA.

Although some mind control slaves are used merely for sex work like Daisy was, that's not really the only thing that this mind control is used for. Most of the time when I was being Kathy, I was socializing with adult Luciferian members of secret societies. The purpose of having me dress in girl's clothing and act feminine wasn't just sexual. It was for depatterning purposes. It was a way to have me break the behavior pattern of ordinary society so that I could be socialized into the Society of Lucifer. It was a way of training me to be a member of a secret society. It wasn't lost on me that people in ordinary society would ridicule any boy who dressed in girl's clothing. And as Kathy, I usually dressed in girl's clothing. But the Luciferians never ridiculed me for dressing in girl's clothing; they complimented me. So I knew that Kathy had to be kept secret and that Kathy's friends had to be kept secret. I was being conditioned to be the faithful keeper of secrets.

The real power of a secret society arises from its ability to remain invisible. Because of its invisibility, it's able to covertly attack people without reprisal. The Illuminati cloak of invisibility makes its criminal actions possible. Much of the sex work I performed on adult men was filmed so they could be blackmailed later. Blackmail, political corruption, financial fraud, bribery and assassination are all methods used by secret societies to achieve power. Secrecy is essential to all of that. Pedophiliac sex work is just one aspect of this criminal matrix.

Even as Kathy I didn't like to do the sex work. It was always scary. Sometimes it was painful. It always made me feel bad. And it was always humiliating. No child enjoys doing sex work. I had been trained to pretend to enjoy it – but even as Kathy, I hated it. I also disliked the Satanic blood rituals. I felt threatened by the ritual torture and killing of animals. All the chanting and spell casting made me feel creepy.

At first I felt uncomfortable dressing up like a girl and acting feminine, but eventually I got used to it. It was a game I played when I was around my Luciferian friends. Children need attention, and this was a way for me to get attention from adults. Most of the time when I socialized with Luciferians I enjoyed talking with them. They were nice to me, mostly. They tutored me in reading and writing. They told me stories. We played card games and ate meals together. They taught me about the philosophy of Luciferianism. And they knew that I would keep secret the fact that they were Luciferians because they would keep secret the fact that I was a boy who sometimes dressed like a girl.

I have talked with other persons recovering from this type of phenomena whereupon your personality becomes bifurcated – that is, a split personality. There is a philosophical question there. Where did this other personality come from? In the case of many people subjected to Satanic Ritual Abuse, the answer is that the other personality is a demon. The question is then, what is a demon? So this is a type of demonic possession, but what is the nature of the demon that is doing the possessing? Is it psychological? Is it religious? Or perhaps does it have something to do with extraterrestrials? I don't know for certain what the answer is to that question concerning the nature of demons. But it is undeniably true that in some sense, demons do in fact exist. And in some cases, the alter personalities involved in the multiple personality phenomena are demons. However demonic possession is not the only explanation for where the alter personalities come from.

I don't believe that I myself became demonically possessed. But certainly there were attempts made to implant me with a demon. Another possible answer to the question of where the alter personality may come from is that it may arise from past-life memories. Many early Christians believed in a form of reincarnation. The name for this phenomena was *gilgul*. They believed that there were certain circumstances where a soul might reincarnate into the world to serve some spiritual purpose. The soul might come back to make atonement for mistakes made in an earlier lifetime. Or a soul might come back on a type of spiritual mission to help humanity at a critical time. I believe that the Kathy personality initially arose from memories of a previous lifetime when I was a woman named Susan the Poisoner. In that incarnation I was a Satanic witch in old Europe who eventually converted to Christianity. And the personality from that lifetime became reactivated when I was subjected to Satanic Ritual Abuse in my present incarnation.

The Kathy personality was always more mature and emotionally stronger than the Kerth personality. The Kathy personality was more physically athletic and more intelligent than the Kerth personality. And perhaps most importantly, the Kathy personality had a much higher tolerance for physical and emotional pain. Kerth could be easily broken, but nobody could break Kathy.

But the Kathy personality was only periodically in control of the body. As Kerth, I was running things most of the time. As Kathy, I could be aware of my life as Kerth – but as Kerth I didn't – couldn't – have any awareness of my life as Kathy. The mind control had created a barrier. This mental barrier protected my normal life as Kerth. But sometimes things came through anyway. I had nightmares and flashbacks. But for a number of years, there was a clear mental barrier between Kathy and Kerth. The trauma-containing memories created a barrier in the memory system. This caused certain memories to be compartmentalized and associated with a certain personality. I was really always only one person. The Kathy personality was one compartment in the memory system, and the Kerth personality was a different compartment. And trauma-containing memories were the bricks used to build the wall that kept these compartments separate.

Trauma-Based Mind Control

I am assuming here that you have heard of mind-control techniques such as MK Ultra, Monarch and Satanic Ritual Abuse. These types of mind control are used by Luciferian secret societies. All of these techniques are really forms of brainwashing which I am going to refer to as trauma-based mind control. The trauma that makes such mind control work is caused by emotional and physical torture. Sometimes it involves drugs. This torture becomes so overwhelming that the experience becomes blocked out of memory. The people who practice this type of trauma-based mind control are very sadistic.

Luciferianism is an occult belief system. Forms of Luciferianism are practiced by the wealthy elite around the globe. These wealthy Luciferians use their secret societies to covertly impose their plans upon the world at large. Trauma-based mind control is one method they use to maintain control over mainstream society.

My goal here is to share enough information that you might have some notion as to what it takes to heal someone suffering from Illuminati mind control. However, I do not intend to share enough information for an unscrupulous amateur, acting alone, to be able to figure out how to use this information to brainwash someone. Nevertheless, covert brainwashing that is highly organized is already being done on a massive scale in society. The Luciferian elite presently have many mind-control technicians with psychiatric training who know perfectly well how to use trauma-based mind control with disturbing skill.

To give an example of how chilling this is, I will describe a film I was once shown. It was a film of the wife of a Senator who had been subjected to trauma-based mind control. The Illuminati's psychiatrists had created an alter personality which could be turned on for the purposes of kinky sex work. In this film of this Senator's wife, I remember that first I could see her normal personality talking with people, and then toward the end of the film, I could see her perform a sex act while she was in her alter personality. This film was in black and white and had sound. It was of reasonable quality for a film shot by an amateur with a handheld camera.

In the first part of the film the Senator's wife is seen visiting the home of a wealthy campaign supporter. He was a man who had donated a great deal of money to her husband's senate campaign. The film had been recorded by the wife of this wealthy supporter using a handheld camera. At the beginning of the film the voice of the camerawoman could be heard more loudly than the voice of the Senator's wife. She was explaining to the Senator's wife that it was an honor to have her there, and they wanted to document the visit in film. The rest of the film was focused on the wealthy contributor himself and the Senator's wife, as he showed her around his estate.

Most of the film was boring. It consisted of the host showing the Senator's wife his big, expensive home with its gardens and such.

The Senator's wife politely compliments him on his home. Then they get out to the stables where this wealthy man keeps his horses. He goes through the expansive stables showing off his horses. Then he takes her outside to a fenced-in area where he shows her his prize stud. She politely admires the horse for a while.

Then this wealthy man says some control phrase to the Senator's wife. Her expression and tone of voice change. He asks her what is her name. She gives a name other than her real name. He orders her to take off all of her clothes and to carefully fold them up and place them on a nearby bench. She systematically strips and carefully places her clothes on the bench. She does this in a very robotic way. So she's standing there naked and showing no emotion. But the wealthy man and his hired hand are sneering at her nude body.

Then he has his hired hand take the bridle of the horse and he orders the Senator's wife to kneel down next to the horse. Then he orders her to start masturbating the horse. The camerawoman, the wealthy contributor and the hired hand all laugh as she robotically does as she's ordered. The horse becomes aroused and eventually ejaculates.

Then the man orders the Senator's to wife redress herself. He has her wash her hands with a hand wipe. Then he brings her back to herself. She rocks back and forth and complains that she blacked out for a second. She complains of a headache. He pretends to be sympathetic. But it's clear that she has no memory of what she's just been forced to do.

The thing is, that everything we experience in life is recorded in the subconscious mind. So the Senator's wife on some level of consciousness did understand what she had been forced to do and could be forced to do at any time. It's also a fact that this Senator's wife was known to develop problems with alcoholism and an addiction to medical drugs. So this manipulation of her personality was not some harmless prank. On some level of consciousness she could feel the humiliation and helplessness of what was done to her.

Furthermore, this film made of her could be used for blackmail purposes. It was a way to guarantee the cooperation of the Senator. It's through such techniques that the government has become so corrupted so that it no longer serves the will of the people. At the present time, the governments in the USA, Israel and Europe only serve a small, wealthy minority of the population. Less than one percent of the population controls the Illuminati-controlled governments. The film of a Senator's wife robotically masturbating a horse was a political event, and she was an innocent mind-control victim.

This type of absolute power appeals to certain types of personalities. It isn't just the perverted sex that appeals to them; it's the power itself. They want to take power from others in order to have that power for themselves. They want to treat people like puppets. They want to program human beings as if they are robots. The eventual goal of these control freaks is world domination.

The Illuminati

In order to understand how mind control works, you have to understand the organization that created the advanced mind-control systems that we now find around the world. You cannot understand the mind-control methodology until you understand the nature of the mind controllers.

The Illuminati is a Luciferian cult – secretive in its organization and dedicated to globalism. I would say that the Bavarian Illuminati that was founded in 1776 is only one of many Luciferian secret societies. In my opinion the Illuminati organization is *not* all powerful, and there are Luciferian cults that are *not* under its complete control. But the word *Illuminati* has also become synonymous with all Satanic activity; it just depends on how the word is used in a sentence. So I believe that it's appropriate to use the word *Illuminati* to either refer to a specific organization called the *Bavarian Illuminati* or to refer to all Luciferian secret societies.

I believe that many people in positions of institutional power in society are actually operatives who work for Luciferian secret societies. But of course, not everyone in a position of wealth and power is a secret society member. Yet most wealthy and powerful persons do know that the Illuminati exists. At the present time, the Illuminati is tolerated by wealthy non-members because it seems to operate for the ultimate benefit of all the wealthiest persons in the world.

This consolidation of power and wealth into the hands of a small group of people is not really a conspiracy theory. For example, in October 2011, the Swiss Federal Institute of Technology conducted a complex study. The scientists who researched the economy detailed how a "Financial Super Entity" was controlling the global economy. The study pointed out how 1% of the companies around the world are controlling 40% of the income. It pointed out how five US banks control half the economy and things have only gotten worse since then. The fact that so much wealth is consolidated into the hands of so few people cannot be a coincidence. The New World Order is a global plutocracy. This global plutocracy was intentionally created and is deliberately maintained. In order to create and maintain such a global plutocracy, a criminal network is required. One way to think about the Illuminati is as the secretive, criminal aspect of this global plutocracy.

Not all of the generationally wealthy families practice Luciferianism. At the elite level of wealth, the most common belief is in some form of Social Darwinism. This means that they think of themselves as genetically superior to those less wealthy than themselves. This is the most popular belief system of those families who have inherited great wealth over numerous generations. They imagine that their so-called superior breeding justifies their wealth. Such beliefs are ridiculous, and the truth is that these people are economic parasites who feed on society without really doing any meaningful work. Yet in spite of their irrational justifications for their own greed, they are not all Satanists.

However, knowingly or unknowingly, all super-wealthy individuals are connected in some way to the Luciferian cults that exist among the generationally wealthy. The Luciferian cults manipulate the most powerful persons in society. You find Luciferian puppets at the top of all important international organizations and governments. Such puppets may not openly refer to themselves as Illuminati; however, whether they call themselves the New World Order or simply the global elite – they are all slaves to Lucifer.

As a discrete organization the Bavarian Illuminati is not all powerful. But it does wield overwhelming power. This official Illuminati organization was originated by Adam Weishaupt on May 1, 1776. This aristocratic Luciferian cult is presently served by a network of criminal organizations, made up of violent Satanists. Almost all organized crime in the USA and Europe is linked to the Illuminati. And they control the governments in the USA, Israel and European Union. They also have relationships with secret societies around the world.

They are presently operating on a schedule for world takeover. They plan to completely collapse the economy of the USA by the end of 2015. They plan to dismantle the federal government of the USA in 2017 to make it a part of a "superstate" that includes Canada and Mexico. They plan to announce their global government in 2020. And they plan to have control of all the resources on the planet Earth by 2050. And thus far, they are on schedule. So the Illuminati members think of themselves as being very powerful.

However, the ultimate puppet-masters are not the Illuminati members. They too are puppets. The ultimate puppet-masters are something more demonic. I have known some very well-educated and well-informed Luciferians who have said that the Illuminati is really being run by some type of hostile extraterrestrial intelligence. I can recall that when I was younger and was involved with the Society of Lucifer. I recall conversations that I had with some Luciferians who believed that they actually were extraterrestrials who were just operating human bodies. They told me this in a very matter-of-fact way. One word for this phenomena is *overshadowing*. The human personality disappears, and the alien/demonic personality overshadows the body and takes it over. Some researchers believe that some aliens are shape-shifters who can take human form. I don't claim to understand everything about these demonic alien overlords. But I do know that the real leaders of the Illuminati aren't really human. Whether or not their DNA is human I don't really know. But I do know that the Illuminati's leaders don't think or behave like human beings, and they don't believe themselves to be human. They actually believe that they are some type of non-human entities. They think and act as if they are some type of intelligent Reptilian creatures.

Some Christian ministers also have become aware of what is going on and are using prayer as a spiritual weapon to challenge these demonic forces. But not all Christian ministries are the same. Some Christians are naive about how the Illuminati works. Some Christian ministers are very narrow-minded and intolerant of those who don't agree with them. But some Christian ministers are very awakened to what is happening with Satanism around the world. And the rise of a global Satanic empire was predicted in Bible prophecy. I have found Christianity and Bible teachings to be personally useful. But I know that not everyone responds to Christianity. In whatever way that you seek to develop your spirituality, you need to have a spiritual awakening. Full spiritual awakening is not just a nice idea, it's a necessity for survival.

Everyone on the planet is interconnected and everyone is psychically influenced by the Illuminati to varying degrees. The victims of Monarch mind control are extreme examples, but the whole of humanity is being influenced by Luciferian psychic driving. So the development of spiritual and psychic awareness is essential to deprogramming Luciferian mind control. Those who are naive about how they are being manipulated fail to realize that they are being driven like sheep to their slaughter.

The wealthy people who know that the Illuminati exists and do nothing to resist it are not really being very smart. They may temporarily have advantages from their wealth, but the Illuminati intends to soon betray those wealthy persons who aren't in the Illuminati. The present plan of the Illuminati is to collapse the economy in the USA completely by the end of 2015. And if the Illuminati continue to get their way, the USA will cease to exist as a sovereign nation by the end of 2017. Although the American people have become naive and decadent, there are still strong cultural memories in the American people of democracy and human rights. So this is why the Illuminati intends to start off their final global depopulation campaign by killing off most Americans. Once the USA is in ruins, the Illuminati plans to attack most of the wealthy families around the world. First they will seize the assets of all wealthy non-Illuminati members and then kill all of them and their families.

Also the Illuminati leaders intend to kill off all loyal Illuminati members and their families as they become non-essential to the Illuminati's plans. So being a loyal Illuminati member is no guarantee of safety. Right now the Illuminati leaders need many loyal members in order to move their plans forward. And so they treat their members well and give them advantages. But they don't trust anyone and they hate all human beings. The Illuminati leaders plan to kill off every human being on the planet except for a few slaves which they intend to severely brainwash. So the Illuminati leaders have policies which will go into effect once they've achieved absolute power and their plan is to kill off anyone in their organization as soon as that member becomes non-essential.

I know a man who is called James the Just by his followers. When I was younger I was involved in a type of resistance movement against the Illuminati, and I sometimes worked with James. One function that he performed was to help Illuminati members escape the cult. In some extreme cases, the members would fake their deaths and assume completely new identities. That was the only way they could leave. So it's very difficult for someone to leave the Illuminati once they have joined.

When I was younger, and also in recent years, I have talked with former members who have escaped the Illuminati. Also I've talked with persons still in the Illuminati but who are disillusioned with it. When members are first recruited they are told that the Illuminati is going to create a utopian world society. But it often becomes obvious to the members when they've been in the group for a while that this utopia is never going to be created. The Illuminati only intends to create a living hell. The Illuminati is really a prison. Its members are prisoners to a cruel and inhuman leadership. And the goal of the Illuminati is to turn the entire world into a never-ending hell-like prison.

Emotional Trauma, Violence & Guilt

It isn't just physical torture that causes people to become traumatized, it's also the emotional trauma that can come from observing the torture of others or being forced to do intensely humiliating things in order to avoid torture. Also most victims feel intense guilt because of their involvement with Satanism even when that involvement is involuntary.

Trauma-based repressed memories tend to fall into one of three categories:

1. Trauma imposed on oneself by an abuser.
2. Witnessing trauma imposed on another by an abuser.
3. Being forced by a controller to impose trauma on someone else.

No matter what category the trauma-containing memories fall into, they tend to create feelings of fear, depression and guilt. Even when the victims of mind control are completely innocent, they tend to feel guilty. And the Satanists like to involve other people in their criminal acts. For example, some victims of mind control are forced to perform animal sacrifice as a way of training them to become Satanists.

The blood rituals performed by some satanic cults are designed to intimidate the cult members. Animal or human sacrifices are performed as a way to psychologically intimidate members of the coven. Those who are forced to observe these rituals always feel intimidated by the displays of violence. Even when these violent rituals are done to animals, observing such rituals can be so emotionally disturbing that the experiences become blocked out of memory.

Also, persons in such cults are sometimes tricked into performing acts of violence. For example, one trick is to torture an animal to death very slowly and then another member who dislikes violence will finally kill the animal in order to stop its suffering. Sometimes victims with multiple personalities will have an alter personality which can be programmed to commit acts of violence.

I once saw a series of movies that showed a man being trained to have multiple personalities, one of which was a trained killer. This man had joined a Satanic criminal cult, but he disliked the violence. Apparently he had joined because he wanted the wealth that came from being involved with it. But a problem arose when his wife found out about the cult. She acquired evidence of their animal and human sacrifices and documented some of their criminal activities. She went to the police, but it turned out that the police officer she reported to was also a Luciferian who was a member of a related coven. So the cult found out what she had done. They abducted her and tortured her to death in front of her husband. They restrained him and made him watch as they raped her and then slowly skinned her alive. Finally she begged them to kill her. At that point, they allowed her husband to kill her. He was weeping as he slit her throat. This experience became the basis for an alter personality which was trained to be a violent enforcer. This alter personality was first trained to torture animals to death and then he was trained to kill people. Eventually this alter personality came to enjoy the violence. It was as if the man was demon possessed and this possession began at the moment when he killed his wife.

In the Illuminati system, those who are in the Satanic criminal cults are trained for violence at a young age. I think I was about ten years old when I was forced to kill a dog. Really it was a puppy. There was a farm that I was sometimes taken to visit with an older relative who was a Satanist. There was a puppy there that I was allowed to play with and feed. After a number of visits, whereupon I had emotionally bonded with the puppy, I was then forced to kill it by drowning it. I didn't want to, but I was told that if I didn't drown it, I would be tortured by being locked in a box. So I killed the puppy. This was considered to be training. Eventually I did escape the cult, but if I had stayed in, I would have been trained to kill people by first being trained to ritualistically kill animals.

Although I've seen movies of human sacrifice, I've never personally witnessed one. But I have personally witnessed quite a few animal sacrifices. The most bizarre and terrifying animal sacrifice I ever saw was the time that the Baron ritualistically killed a chimpanzee. He had the chimp dressed up like a minister. The chimp wore a cross around his neck. Apparently the chimp cost the Baron a lot of money. So it was unusual to see a chimp used in animal sacrifice. The Baron had this whole ritual filmed as some type of Satanic training film.

This took place in the basement of his mansion that had been set up as a Satanic temple. He had a large basement underneath his mansion. It had all been painted black. It was lit with gas lights, no electric lights. This gave it a weird glow. There were strange mystical markings on the floor that were painted in red. And there was an altar at one end of the basement. For this ritual he had gathered some of his followers there. Most of them were dressed in black robes with hoods. They were naked underneath the robes.

Although I was a boy, the Baron liked to make me dress up in girl's clothing. For this ritual, I was dressed up all in red. I had on a red dress, red stockings, red boots and red hair. I had on plastic red horns that came up out of my head. I held a plastic red trident. The makeup that had been put on my face made it look reddish. When I looked in the mirror I looked like a devil. And this scared me. When we went down to the Baron's basement temple I was the only person dressed like this, everyone else had on black robes.

Then this whole ritual was filmed with multiple cameras. The Baron brought the unsuspecting chimp into the room and walked him around, introducing him to his coven members as Mr. Christian Minister. The chimp was dressed in a minister's shirt and collar with a cross symbol hanging from a cord around his neck. The chimp looked old and seemed weakened somehow. But he had been trained to interact with people. The chimp shook hands with people and they chuckled. But then the humor of the situation ended abruptly when the Baron had the Chimp tied down to a table. It took four men to do this and it was quite an accomplishment. The chimp bit the men and was screaming and chattering the whole time. Once this was accomplished, the Baron put on a mask that made him look like a demon. He stuck a ritual knife into one corner of the table and told his audience that anyone who wanted to could slit the throat of "Mr. Christian Minister" at any time. Then the Baron slowly tortured the chimp in different ways. It was agonizing to watch this. It was the worse animal sacrifice I'd ever seen. And the chimp screeched and chattered in overwhelming pain the whole time. Finally I took the knife and slit his throat just to stop his pain. I just couldn't stand to see this innocent animal in so much pain.

After I killed the chimp, the Baron had me stand up on his altar holding the bloody knife in one hand. The Baron began to bow down and worship me. Then everyone else joined him.

They chanted, "Blessed is the anti-Christ who shall destroy the doomed Christian Church."

I looked down at them and then over at the dead Chimp. Suddenly everything in the room took on an orange glow. I suddenly felt an intense pain in my solar plexus, and I felt that there was a powerful evil presence in the room. I began to cry. Without thinking about it I cut my left arm three times. The cuts weren't so deep that I bled to death, but they were bad cuts and I still have faint scars from them. The Baron immediately stopped the filming of me. I climbed off the altar and went into a catatonic state for a while. I was aware of what was happening around me but I was completely non-responsive.

A few hours later I came out of it. By then I had been cleaned up and put back into my boy's clothing. My left arm had been bandaged. Apparently I hadn't lost so much blood that I needed to go to the hospital. I was on a couch in the Baron's downstairs library. Bob's sister Betsy had one arm around me and was holding a Bible that she had gotten from the Baron's reference library. She was reading out loud from the Bible. She had multiple personalities and she had gone from her Satanist sex worker personality into an alter Christian personality.

Somebody later explained to me that the Baron had gone on with his film using a different boy who they had dressed up as I had been. Different men and women had sex with the boy and then worshiped him as if he were the anti-Christ. The Baron apparently intended that the spirit of the anti-Christ would possess me, to speak through me to the coven. The Baron was upset because I had wrecked his magickal working when I cut myself. But he could still sell the movie of this event to other wealthy Satanists because of the entertainment value of the torture and the sexual content.

I don't ever recall that the Baron himself performed human sacrifices or allowed others in his coven to do so. For some reason he drew the line at performing human ritual sacrifice, although he seemed to have committed every other sin of which he could possibly conceive. Apparently the Baron got the idea for this odd ritual in which he tortured the chimp from something that was done in England. The story was that a ritual like the one I've described was performed by some members of British royalty, only they used an actual Christian minister instead of a chimp. And after the boy in the red dress killed the minister, he became possessed by a demon. He stood up on the altar and started speaking to his coven in different languages, describing a plan to destroy all Christianity.

The thing that's odd about all this was that the Baron was a Christian. When he wasn't being a Satanist, he lived his life as a Christian. Someone who knew him better than me said that he took his Christianity very seriously. The Baron didn't have multiple personalities. His Christian personality could remember everything that his Satanist personality did. I don't think that the Baron believed what most Christians believe, but he did believe in the power of ceremonial rituals. The Baron apparently actually believed that being a Christian and performing Christian rituals meant that all his sins would be forgiven when he died. So the idea was that he could use his Satanism to make himself wealthy in the world and still go to Heaven when he died – as unlikely as that sounds.

I've known a number of Satanists who were also Christians. They believed that the sins that they committed as Satanists could be forgiven by Christ, so they took Christian beliefs and practices seriously. Satanism is like a drug to which a person becomes addicted. This addiction is to the worldly power and wealth that can come from satanic practices. Also some Satanists claim that they get feelings of glee when they worship Satan. Some practitioners feel that they can't stop. But some Satanists also feel bad about what they've done and pray to Christ for forgiveness.

Personally I don't think that it's enough to just perform some type of religious ritual and assume that this will make up for all wrongdoings. I don't believe in the authority of any religion. But I am aware of the existence of God the Creator, and I do believe in the authority of God. I do believe that the true nature of God is forgiveness. I have known some Satanists and former Satanists who have made acts of atonement to prepare themselves spiritually to accept God's grace. The greatest act of atonement that one can make is to do something significant to oppose the Illuminati and to undermine its plans.

There is a spiritual entity I identify as Christ. I think that there can be other names for this redeeming spirit, but the name I personally use is Christ. I believe that all of my transgressions have been forgiven by Christ. I am grateful that Christ has healed me.

And for the record, I'm not really the anti-Christ, it was just some stupid film the Baron made. I say this because I know that some Illuminati members have seen the Baron's film of me being worshipped as the anti-Christ. But I didn't accept the demonic presence during that ritual – I just went catatonic for a while. And I do completely renounce Satan, Lucifer and the anti-Christ.

There is a divine supreme being. There have been many different names for this divine source of creation. Whatever name you use for this Divine Grace, you must allow yourself to be filled with it. A demon can only possess you if you have a spiritual emptiness in your heart. Allowing yourself to be filled with Divine Grace frees you from the vulnerability of demonic possession.

I point this out because I feel that a developed spirituality is necessary to mental health and to deprogramming mind control. A developed spirituality heals emotional trauma. And a spiritual relationship with the Divine Source can free you from the feelings of guilt that may come from being involved with a satanic group. Different people approach spirituality in different ways, and everyone has to find their own path. For me, Christianity has been an important part of my personal path. But it's important to distinguish the difference between spirituality and religion. Some people are religious without being spiritual, and a person can be spiritual without being religious. Nonetheless, it's the spirituality that really matters. And religious dogma can be a terrible barrier to authentic spirituality.

Exorcism & Catholicism

I don't claim to understand exactly how every branch of the Illuminati is structured. But some of my experiences as a child prostitute seem to indicate that there is a branch of the Illuminati which controls the Catholic Church. Also there seems to be a branch of the Illuminati that influences other Christian institutions. And there are branches of the Illuminati which control some Islamic sects as well as the Zionists. However, from what I've been told by insiders, Satanism goes back in the Catholic Church for centuries. A Catholic priest, with whom I had a sexual relationship for a while when I was a boy, once explained to me that there are actually two Catholic churches woven together into one institution.

There is the openly known Catholic Church and the Shadow Church. A priest may be a Christian priest, but he may also be a Satanic priest as well. Only a minority of priests and nuns in the Catholic Church are in this Shadow Church. Most Catholics are clueless when it comes to this Shadow Church. But the Shadow Church is what really runs the Catholic Church. I'm not saying that all Catholics are really Satanists. The Illuminati system is really controlling all branches of society in Western Civilization. The control of the Illuminati is top down. So the Catholic Church is not an exception to that control. The leaders of the United States federal government are Illuminati puppets just like the leaders of the Catholic Church are Illuminati puppets. But the average American isn't a Satanist and the average Catholic isn't one either. Yet the Catholic Church seems to be more under the thumb of Satanists than other forms of Christianity. The Catholic Church isn't unique in this, at this time Israel is also very much under the thumb of Satanists. I'm not trying to put down anyone's spirituality, but certain religious institutions are very much obsessed with using mind control on their members, and the Catholic Church is one of them. I've attended mass a number of times with Catholic friends, and I believe that it can be a very spiritual experience. For some people, the spirituality of Catholicism is a meaningful experience, but as a theocratic institution, the Catholic Church is very much controlled by secretive Satanists.

I don't know if this is true of all priests in the Shadow Church, but the ones I've known seemed very obsessed with anilingus. This is a sex act where one person kisses and licks the anus of another person. I was forced to perform this dozens of times when I was a child, and it always felt shaming to do this. This might be the point of the ritual: that this is not so much a sexual ritual as it is a ritual which is supposed to make the participants feel ashamed. The anilingus ritual, as I was taught it, was always performed in this way. First, the man's anus was carefully cleaned with two dishrags using two bowls of warm water. First the the anus would be cleaned out with warm soapy water, then with warm water which had no soap in it. The cleaning out of the anus had to be done slowly and very carefully. Then a clear plastic sheet of the type of wrapping paper that is used to preserve food would be utilized. Saran wrap or that type of thing. This would be fitted into the butt crack and spread across the man's buttock. Anilingus would then be performed by sticking ones tongue into the anus as far as possible and kissing the anus repeatedly. My pimp, Bob, was obsessed with avoiding sexually transmitted diseases, so this method of anilingus may have been more hygienic than what was typical. I point this out because according to what I've been told, in the Shadow Church, rituals involving anilingus are considered to be very important. And I can tell you from personal experience that such rituals are demeaning and grotesque. So this speaks to the nature of the Shadow Church.

The Shadow Church which runs the Catholic Church is older than the Illuminati. I've been told that the Satanic Shadow Church first infiltrated the Catholic Church leadership in the eighth or ninth century. However, this Shadow Church was never all powerful. In order to maintain its invisibility, it had to maintain a low profile and work in subtle ways to manipulate the Church. However, over the centuries, this Shadow Church has become increasing influential. But as the Illuminati grew in power, this Shadow Church was eventually absorbed into it. Now the Satanic Shadow Church which runs Vatican City is merely another branch of the Illuminati. Vatican City isn't really Christian anymore, it's now just another center of Illuminati power like Washington DC, Las Vegas and the Financial District in the City of London.

This point needs to be made because the Catholic Church has promoted completely misleading ideas about demonic exorcism. If you can accept that demons do exist, and that they can be exorcised, then you should know Catholic exorcism is totally ineffective. The movies which glorify the Catholic Church's way of exorcism always depict a priest doing war with a demon. This is done by tying up the demon-possessed person after which the priest recites verses in Latin. In the movies, supernatural horrors are depicted before the demon is finally sent back to hell and the demon-possessed person is freed. But the truth is that tying up a person and chanting verses in Latin or any other language would actually only be another form of mind control. This is not true exorcism, it's just more brainwashing.

The stories in the Bible of Jesus freeing people from demons never involve him tying anyone up or chanting verses in Latin. So I have to say that Catholic exorcism likely doesn't work and may be harmful. However things like simple faith in the Divine and sincere prayer work miracles. And there have been reports of some Catholic priests who have some success with persons who appeared to be demon possessed. However, this doesn't verify the power of the Catholic exorcism rituals. It only confirms that faith and prayer in general can be very powerful. So there is no excuse for tying people up as part of an exorcism ritual. And there is nothing particularly spiritual about Latin. The historical Christ never spoke it, and it's not a sacred language. Ancient Rome may have been the most Satanic empire in the history of the world, the idea that its language is sacred or has spiritual power is absurd. If anything, Latin is the language of demons, not the language of angels.

Demons are the spirits of hostile entities. These demons overshadow human beings who have been subjected to trauma-based mind control.

Personally I like to read and reread the stories in the Bible of Jesus expelling demons. The use of trauma-causing mind control was very common in the regions controlled by the Roman Empire during the time of the historical Jesus. This practice of trauma-causing mind control was common in the cults known as Mystery Schools. The Mystery Schools were for the aristocrats, but other cults found among the common people used the same techniques. What the Bible refers to as a demon is what a psychologist would refer to as an alter personality. This is a symptom of a person suffering with multiple personality disorder (MPD). So when the Bible tells stories of Jesus releasing people from demons, realize that this may not just be a mythological story. The historical man, upon whom the story of Jesus was based, was someone who was releasing people from the effects of ancient brainwashing cults. Christ, the historical Jesus, was a deprogrammer.

Toxic Therapy Systems

Before I go further into how this Fabian system works, I want to contrast it to what is going on with the therapy systems presently available in society. It may be difficult to convey this point but many of these therapeutic institutions are covertly designed to do harm to their patients. Psychiatry is intentionally designed to make people insane and keep them that way. Psychology in general is designed to not cure anyone but to make people dependent upon psychologists. Medical practice is designed to occasionally heal people, but to also do things which make them sick and dependent upon the medical system. All of the therapy systems available in society are intentionally designed to be somewhat toxic.

When I was young I knew that there were Satanic secret societies among the wealthy. And some of the people I knew who were involved with these would say that someday the Luciferians were going to take over the world. Back in those days, I found that idea unlikely. But now that I understand more about how the institutions in society are organized, I realize that this was not an idle boast.

After World War Two the United States tried to take possession of the intellectual resources of Nazi Germany. The CIA created Project Paperclip, brought former Nazi scientists into the United States and made them into citizens. This fact of history has been sold to the American public as a wonderful thing. The apologists for Project Paperclip point out that Warner Von Braun was one of these Nazi Paperclip heros, and that he created the space program which allowed us to go to the Moon. But none of these Ex-Nazis were heros, and the reality of what Project Paperclip really did was hideously destructive.

The MK Ultra program for mind control was driven in a large part by Nazi scientists. The MK stands for Mind Kontrolle, the English word for mind and the German word for control. Think about this. Who's really in *Kontrolle*? Obviously the Nazis are. The Nazis were a creation of the Illuminati. The Nazi Party was a project run by the Bavarian Illuminati. The German people were defeated by the Allied Forces at the end of World War Two. But the Nazis were never defeated. They were transferred from Germany into positions of power in the United States and elsewhere.

In the United States former Nazis and other Illuminati stooges were put in positions of power to undermine the use of certain institutions. The medical profession and other so called institutions of therapy have been engineered to do harm instead of healing. I'm not saying that all doctors and psychologists are evil. They have been educated and deceived like everyone else. Doctors and psychologists take up their professions hoping to become healers. But they are subtlety mislead during their educational process. The institutions of medicine, psychology and psychiatry have all been engineered to have some healing potential but to also do some harm. In some cases, such as psychiatry, hospital birth and circumcision, the harm done is very great. And it is intentionally evil.

But Fabian Therapy was never designed like that. The therapists who designed this system were disillusioned Illuminati insiders. They rejected the Illuminati plan to create a toxic therapy system. The Fabians actually designed their therapy system to do no harm and to heal their clients as quickly as possible. They intended that their clients be independent and empowered.

Fabian Technique

I should warn you that if you have been subjected to Illuminati mind control, my message here may trigger negative feelings in you. You may feel lightheaded, or you may even feel angry or afraid. I would encourage you to remain sensitive to your feelings as you consider what I am communicating.

What I am describing here is an approach to therapy that is probably different than what you've heard of before. Over the years I have had access to certain insider information which I am sharing with you. I was subjected to Satanic Ritual Abuse as a child, and some of my abusers had psychiatric training and were experimenting with the beginnings of what would lead to Monarch-type mind control. I never completely fell under the complete influence of this type of mind control, but it created many problems for me. I had many personal problems and emotional health issues that arose from having been subjected to this abuse against my will. Later on, I was helped by some people who had backgrounds in psychology, people who had developed a technique for healing this type of mind control. I received help from this type of therapy and I have known others who were helped by it.

The scientists who actually developed this system had a rather technical name for it, but I simply call this technique, *Fabian Therapy*. This is because the scientists who developed this therapy system believed that persons who have been brutalized with trauma-based mind control are best treated with what may be thought of as a Fabian-type strategy for therapy. This type of strategy is named for a Roman General. In Fabian Strategy you avoid a direct, frontal, military assault and instead you gradually wear down your opponent over time by using indirect attacks. This type of military strategy was used by General Washington to defeat the British, by the Russians to defeat Napoleon and by Sam Houston to defeat Santa Anna. This strategy works only in situations where you have time on your side and the discipline to maintain a continual attack which slowly weakens your opponent. It has also been used in non-military situations. Corporations sometimes use this approach to defeat competitors. The British Fabian Society is attempting to use this type of strategy to promote its socialist agenda. The Illuminati itself is attempting to use a Fabian Strategy to conquer the world. Although the Illuminati's intentions are evil, a Fabian Strategy in itself is morally neutral – what you choose to do with it determines whether it is good or evil.

The scientists and psychologists who developed this Fabian Therapy system were Illuminati insiders who had become disillusioned with the Illuminati. The Illuminati likes to recruit persons who are idealistic and well-educated. It does this by telling them that when it takes over the world the Illuminati will create a utopian world government. Most who join the secretive Illuminati start off believing that they are going to change the world for the better. However as they learn what is really going on, some Illuminati members figure out that the leaders of their movement are really only interested in making themselves wealthier and more powerful. The disillusioned Illuminati members, who helped me, had come to realize that trauma-based mind control methods are insanely cruel and destructive. So they used their insider information to come up with a system for deprogramming trauma-based mind control.

The victims of trauma-based mind control are programmed with commands that are implanted into their subconscious minds. These implanted commands are designed to keep the victims under control. These commands are precisely worded statements that are given to the victim when he or she is in an altered state of mind. This altered state makes the victim highly receptive to suggestion.

Implanted commands instruct the victim that he or she is unable to consciously remember having been programmed. Sometimes implanted commands are given which instruct these mind control victims to attack anyone who tries to deprogram them. Implanted commands are also sometimes given which instruct them to commit suicide if they start to remember what happened. And even without implanted commands, the depressing nature of this type of abuse can make the victims feel suicidal when they start to recall the abuse. All of this makes therapy for such victims very difficult.

Psychologists have long recognized the phenomenon of repressed memory. This is a type of selective amnesia. A painful experience which threatens the ego of the individual becomes repressed from normal recall. Implanted commands are contained in a type of repressed memory, but trauma-based repressed memories are harder to deal with than the repressed memories the average therapist encounters.

The human mind has a type of defense mechanism. If an experience is too painful or upsetting, the individual represses it from conscious memory so that he can go on with life. This natural defense system allows the individual to continue to function in society even in the wake of an upsetting experience. Traditional therapy methods often try to confront such repressed memories by using hypnosis or other methods which encourage the patient to remember. This is like a direct, or frontal attack on repressed memories. Fabian Therapy is different.

Fabian Therapy avoids direct contact with painful memories. It does not try to expose repressed memories which might trigger implanted commands. It uses an indirect approach that works gradually over a long period of time. It's based on an advanced scientific understanding of the human mind.

But in a sense, Fabian Therapy is more than just a technique; it's an attitude for life. The idea is that instead of trying to confront and re-experience traumatic events, you teach yourself to focus on the present time and environment. You develop an attitude of love and serenity which you express in your present-time environment. When negative feelings or compulsions arise from the past – you have techniques for processing them. That way, you don't get drawn into the trauma from the past.

Fabian Lifestyle & Attitude

The Fabian therapists didn't just develop a technique for healing trauma-based mind control. They had a philosophy for life and an attitude for living which they promoted to their clients. There were two well-known reference books that they encouraged their clients to read. These were *Games People Play* by Eric Berne and *I'm OK, You're OK* by Thomas Anthony Harris.

Both books are based in part on the research of a brain surgeon named Wilder Penfield. He sometimes stimulated small areas of the brain and in doing so he would evoke clear and random memories in his patients. They would find themselves reliving experiences from years earlier. This recall would be vivid. These experiments led Penfield and other researchers to the conclusion that everything we experience is recorded in memory, whether or not we can easily recall such experiences.

Gestalt psychologists analyze social transactions as having three basic viewpoints: *parent, adult* and *child*. The *parental* point of view is controlling and judgmental. The *child* point of view rejects personal responsibility. But the *adult* point of view is that of self responsibility and mutual respect. The contention is that within all memories of social interactions these viewpoints can be perceived. And the idea is to overcome the temptation to assume a parental or childlike viewpoint so that you can center your life in the adult viewpoint.

The Fabian therapists had a similar but somewhat different way of analyzing the memories contained in trauma-based experiences. In every trauma-based memory there are four viewpoints: *abuser, enabler, victim* and *survivor*. The *abuser* is the person or persons causing the abuse to happen. The *enabler* is anyone who cooperates with the abuser. The *victim* is the person who receives the abuse. And the *survivor* is the recovered victim who was able to process the abuse and is no longer influenced by it. Also the survivor is the point of view a victim needs to

Mental Liberation

assume so that the abuse can be survived. Of course, depending upon the incident, there may be many abusers and many victims. What the Fabian therapists were concerned with was the perception of abuse and victimhood.

Capture bonding is a phenomena recognized by psychologists. This takes place when prisoners begin to admire, worship or identify with their abusive captors. This same thing can happen when victims begin to admire and identify with their abusers. The Fabian therapists would have their clients avoid direct contact with trauma-containing memories. But they were aware that these memories still had a subconscious influence on their clients. So they knew that their clients might have a subconscious identification with abusive personalities. So the victims of trauma-based mind control might act out abusively in various ways. When the therapists saw that a client was becoming abusive in some way in his life, they would know that this might represent an identification with an abusive personality.

As a teenager and in my early twenties, I could be very verbally abusive and I would also sometimes shoplift and things like that. So I was what they called a juvenile offender. My therapists helped me to understand why I was acting out in these destructive ways.

The point of Fabian Therapy is to overcome any temptation to identify with the abuser or the enabler. Rather than going into the painful memories and figure which abusive personality I was identifying with, the Fabian therapist looked at what they called the *transactions* between other people and me. These transactions are the social interactions of ordinary communication. The therapists would analyze how I communicated with them in the therapy sessions. But we would also talk about how I communicated with friends and girlfriends in situations outside of therapy. The therapists would use books like *Games People Play* to educate their clients on the difference between healthy transactions and unhealthy ones.

Even without trying to directly recall trauma-containing memories, the behavior of abusive personalities would sometimes subtlety surface in the behavior of a client. For example, the Baron had the habit of snapping his fingers when he was ordering people around. He apparently had gone to a boarding school out East or in England, and at times he affected a type of aristocratic and snobbish manner of speaking. In therapy, if I started snapping my fingers, ordering people around or talking in an affected voice, it was an indication that I was identifying with the Baron. If I started doing that when I was talking with them, they had several ways of dealing with that. One was to do a deliberate "mirroring" of speech and behavior. First the therapist would indicate that he was going to imitate what I had just said. Then he would mimic what I had just said in the manner I had just said it, using my exact words. This way I could see that I was identifying myself with a personality not my own.

The therapists also often tape-recorded sessions and would play back recordings at times for that purpose. Toward the end of the time I was working with them, they began to film sessions and sometimes playback conversations. Also they would sometimes get me to reconnect with my primary personality by asking me about my basic values. For example, if I described a situation where I was verbally abusive with my girlfriend, they might ask me how I would feel if somebody talked to me in that way. And they would ask whether or not I felt that it was OK for people to deliberately hurt the feelings of others. Usually such conversations would move my attention away from the point of view of an abusive personality and back to that of my non-abusive, natural core personality.

The other dynamic of Fabian Therapy is to transcend the attitude of victimhood in order to achieve the attitude of survivorship. That means that you have to focus in on the positive experiences in life and create a positive life for yourself. You don't want to dwell just on the unhappy experiences and the wrongness of having been abused. This is not an approach to therapy where you dwell on every little thing that ever went wrong with your life. You focus on the happy experiences and you bring them fully into your consciousness.

The Fabian therapists were empathetic without being sympathetic. They would acknowledge the abuse and the wrongness of such abuse, but they wouldn't let you dwell on it. This is particularly important for trauma-based mind control victims. Once you go into the pain and humiliation of the abuse, it's a deep pit of despair. And if you fall into deep despair, suicide or drug addiction can be the result. So you have to deal with the negative memories of trauma-based mind control appropriately – as if the memories are no more than garbage to be thrown out. The Fabian therapists taught me a cathartic methods by which negative emotions can be processed and released. For example, if I felt anger for no rational reason, it probably had a source in repressed memories of trauma. Instead of going into the repressed memory, the Fabian therapists might have me beat on a drum in a way that expressed my anger as a way of releasing it energetically.

But these Fabian therapists didn't want their clients to dwell on anything negative. Instead, they encouraged their clients to create positive experiences and to fully embrace these positive experiences.

Exceptions
to the Fabian Therapy Approach

I've said that the Fabian therapists tended to avoid having the client go into painful memories from the past and instead encouraged a rehabilitation of the memory system. However, there were always exceptions. They were experts on the use of hypnosis. They knew how to use hypnosis to place a client in a trance state where he or she would be receptive to suggestion. And they knew how to use hypnotic suggestions to protect the client from the pain contained in trauma-related memories. But they only did this in emergency situations. Sometimes a crisis in a client's life required that the therapists find information which could only be acquired through hypnosis.

However, they used hypnosis as seldom as possible. Because they could stabilize my life and help me without using hypnotherapy, I never experienced the use of hypnotherapy to recover suppressed memories of traumatic experiences. But they did sometimes use hypnotherapy with other clients. They might use it to find out critical information, or they might make posthypnotic suggestions to the effect that a client's life would become more stable. They might use hypnosis to help a client withdraw from dangerous recreational drugs that were making the client's life unstable. They might use hypnosis to help a client with a health crisis. But their basic rule of thumb was to use hypnosis as little as possible and only when necessary.

I suppose their reasoning for this attitude was that their clients had already been manipulated through harsh mind-control methods. They wanted their clients to regain self determinism. For the client to become dependent upon the therapists through hypnosis would go against that goal. So they were very thoughtful about when and how they used hypnotic techniques.

I have known some persons who used hypnotherapy to help themselves recover lost memories which were due to trauma-based mind control. And I have known some persons to have gotten positive results from hypnotherapy. But there are certain warnings that must be given if you, or someone you know, is thinking about employing a hypnotherapist. Some hypnotherapists are very unethical and can cause harm. Others are skillful, ethical and trustworthy. Here are some guidelines: Any therapist who will not tell you up front how he works should not be trusted. Therapists with secret methods which they don't share publicly should not be trusted. Any therapy group that wants to get you alone into a remote environment which they control is not to be trusted. However, ethical therapists will be happy to openly explain how they work. An ethical therapist will not object to you having someone you trust be with you during the session. And you should bring a trusted friend with you if you decide to pursue hypnotherapy. They can sit quietly in the room with you and observe while the session is going on. An ethical therapist will not object to the hypnotherapy session being recorded. Ethical therapists will have offices in relatively public areas where an abduction would not be easy. You really can't be too careful.

One problem is that the Illuminati has set up front organizations which claim to be opposed to the Illuminati but which are actually looking for Illuminati defectors and others who might cause problems for the Illuminati. Some of these Illuminati front groups claim to be Christians. Some of these Illuminati front groups claim to be anti-cult groups. If you have been the victim of Illuminati mind control, and you get involved with one of these groups, they will create problems for you at the very least. So developing a sense of discernment is important.

But if you are looking for help, there are those who will help you. There is a quiet industry that is emerging which is made up of psychologists and hypnotherapists who treat the victims of trauma-based mind control. This is sometimes dangerous for the therapists. So usually they don't advertise the fact that they do this. You will need to study hypnotherapy and interview anyone you hire to help you if you choose this path of using hypnotherapy to recover lost memories. One thing is for certain: *it is very difficult to face these painful memories if you are completely alone*. So you have to think carefully about whom you are going to turn to in order to seek help.

Unfortunately, at this time, those who seek to heal the victims of trauma-based mind control face a great deal of opposition as they try to organize themselves. But those who inflict trauma-based mind control on innocent victims are highly organized, and they have roots that go back into ancient times.

A Brief History of Trauma-Based Mind Control

Before I describe the details of Fabian Therapy I want to go over some other information related to Luciferian mind control. At the time of my birth, Satanic Ritual Abuse was really more of an art form than a science.

The roots of this form of mind control go back to the Mystery Schools which existed in ancient Greece and Rome. The goal of the Mystery Schools was to train each student to accept the guidance of a daemon, which was conceived of as a type of a supernatural spirit. But these daemons were really just demons. And these Mystery Schools would turn their students into arrogant aristocrats who manipulated their subjects.

Although this movement has ancient roots, the contemporary forms of Luciferianism were first developed in Medieval Europe; and they were based on occultism and demonology. Demonic possession is the goal of traditional Satanic Ritual Abuse. The idea of these rituals is that the ordinary personality of a child is to be replaced with a demonic personality that has occultic powers. Sometimes the word magick, spelt deliberately with a "k", is used as a reference to occult ceremonial rituals. Satanists believe that they are magickally empowering a child by subjecting him to demonic possession.

The Luciferians I knew when I was young would sometimes refer to non-Luciferians as being *mundane*. According to this special Luciferian definition of the word, a person who is mundane has no occultic power. Also a mundane person has no access to secret Luciferian knowledge. In this sense, although I am not a Luciferian, I am not entirely mundane because I do have some understanding of hidden Luciferian knowledge.

On a personal note, the woman who first subjected me to Satanic Ritual

Abuse was named Shotzy. She spoke with a German accent and had long black hair that she wore in a bun on top of her head. She had psychiatric training and practiced a form of Satanism. I have reason to believe that she had once been a member of the Vril Society, that she had once dabbled in Theosophy, but eventually she graduated to a form of hard core Satanism influenced by the writings of Aleister Crowley.

In Satanic Ritual Abuse a child is traumatized with rape and torture until the mundane personality disappears and a demonic personality takes over. Programs such as MK Ultra were developed to turn Satanic Ritual Abuse from an intuitive craft into an exacting technology.

The CIA is managed by the Skull and Bones Society – and the Skull and Bones Society is a branch of the Illuminati. After the second World War the CIA recruited Nazi psychiatrists – war criminals – and brought them to the U.S. with Operation Paperclip. It was Satanists in the CIA who funded the early scientific studies of mind control. Although it was eventually disbanded, many MK Ultra-type mind control methods are still in use. These contemporary mind control systems are sometimes administered by psychiatrists in hospital settings. They are much more effective than the earlier experimental programs such as the ones done by Donald Ewen Cameron and the early LSD researchers. Monarch mind control is one such contemporary program. It's known to have been used on some Hollywood celebrities and music stars, as well as many other victims. The Illuminati has psychiatrists specially trained in mind control, and their techniques are very successful in brainwashing people.

THE PROCESS OF
TRAUMA-BASED MIND CONTROL

The victim of Monarch programming may be called a *slave*. He or she is controlled by a person who may be known as an owner, handler or master. The *core personality* is the authentic personality that the victim had before being subjected to mind control. Monarch programming attacks this core personality so that a new personality can be programmed in. The slave is subjected to trauma which causes the core personality to disassociate.

Disassociation takes place when a person becomes disconnected from reality. In such a state the person can be reeducated with new values and motivations. The processes that Illuminati psychiatrists use to do this are very exact. A mischievous amateur experimenting with brainwashing would probably not be able to duplicate their results in some simple way. If you simply render someone unconscious and repeat commands in his presence, it's probable that those commands would never be obeyed. The procedure for implanting commands has other dynamics of psychology which I don't feel comfortable sharing with the general public. I can tell you that the contemporary forms of Illuminati mind control are very sophisticated. The procedures used by these Illuminati psychiatrists are an exacting form of psychic surgery where the individual's psyche is dissected. This creates a new personality that is compartmentalized from the core personality. And it is trauma-based disassociation which builds the walls of this compartmentalization.

Some forms of torture that are used to create this trauma necessary to disassociation are sensory deprivation, confinement, restraints, near drowning, hot and cold extremes, spinning, being hung upside down and being psychologically tormented. Most of these techniques are designed to avoid leaving physical bruises or scars. Shotzy was an expert at torturing children with techniques that didn't leave physical bruises. I remember a technique that Shotzy used on me and other children which simulated drowning. With the help of her assistants, she would wrap her victim up in a sheet and to repeatedly dunk his or her head into a bathtub filled with water. This was like an awkward form of waterboarding. In trauma-based mind control, often family and friends are threatened as a form of psychological torment. As a child I was frequently told that my mother would be killed if I ever talked. That certainly gave me a motivation to keep my abusers' secrets.

It's common in Satanic abuse that bizarre visual elements are included in the sessions to give them a surrealistic feeling. This makes any disclosure by the victim seem non-credible. For example, when I was a child, one of my programmers would always wear a Halloween Frankenstein mask. One morning, after a night of witnessing Satanic rituals, I told my mother that my nanny, Shotzy, had taken me away to see the Frankenstein monster. My mother convinced me that it had all just been a nightmare and that I should forget it. It was because of this type of deceptive techniques that my parents, who were not themselves in the Illuminati, were never aware of the fact that me and my siblings were being subjected to abuse.

As well as this, *control symbols* are used to keep victimized children in line. Mind control commands are associated with a visual symbol so that when the victim sees this symbol, the implanted command with which it is associated will be reinforced. These elaborate methods of psychological manipulation keep anyone victimized by Illuminati mind control from disclosing or even remembering the traumatic experiences.

For example, when I was a child, to keep me from telling others about the abuse I was receiving, one thing that was done to me was that Shotzy took me to a remote location where she performed a Satanic ritual with a live cat and two teddy bears. All three were trussed up in exactly the same fashion on three crosses. The live cat was systematically tortured to death. Every thing that was done to the cat was subsequently done to one of the teddy bears. After a needle was stuck into the cat's arm, a needle was stuck into the arm of the teddy bear next to him. But the other teddy bear was always left alone. When Shotzy finally got around to tearing out the intestines of the living cat, she then in turn tore out some of the stuffing from in the stomach of the teddy bear. And Shotzy went on like this, going back and forth until the cat was dead. But the other teddy bear was left completely unharmed. After I endured this intimidating demonstration of torture techniques, suggestions were made to me that I would not remember this experience. Then when my nanny, Shotzy, brought me back home after our field trip (which my parents believed was a trip to the zoo) she made a point of giving me the unharmed teddy bear as a present. She did this in front of my unsuspecting parents who insisted that I thank her for the gift. The idea was that the teddy bear would act as a subconscious symbolic trigger to condition me so that I could not tell anyone what was being done to me.

My parents were very please to see that Shotzy, my nanny, had given me a teddy bear as a gift. They were very surprised when two days later I burnt it up in the fireplace. Although I didn't ever find a way to tell my parents what was being done to me, I did find ways to rebel against Shotzy.

In many respects my own Satanic Ritual mind control was botched because this was back in the early 1960s when the Illuminati were still experimenting with new methodologies, and my Illuminati programers disagreed about how to program me – sometimes they would even argue about this in front of me. Some aristocratic Illuminati members were interested in my bloodlines. Some of these aristocrats thought I might have the potential to become a leader in their organization, and they didn't want me overly damaged. They ultimately decided that Shotzy's techniques were too experimental and not traditional enough – and so she was dismissed as my controller. This meant that some of these processes of mind control that had been used on me were left incomplete. Most victims of mind control come to believe that resistance is futile, and they give up trying. But I never completely gave up resisting because sometimes I was able to do so successfully.

In those days, Illuminati mind control was half occultic art and half science, but contemporary Monarch mind control is really more like a precise technology. It's unlikely that a Monarch slave will come out of the mind control on his or her own. Monarch slaves are often used for prostitution, assassination, and as message couriers. They are also used in the Illuminati-controlled mass media as celebrities or news personalities. The sexual orientation of the slave can be changed from straight to gay, or gay to straight, or whatever. The slave's owner or master has certain phrases by which he can trigger his slave's programming to control that person. The ultimate goal of Illuminati mind control is to develop a psychiatric technology for destroying free will in humans. Free will is a God-given gift, and as Satanists, they desire to rebel against God in all ways.

A lightheadedness is associated with Monarch mind control, which is one reason that it is named for a butterfly. This process of mind control results in the deliberate creation of Multiple Personality Disorder (MPD) also known as Dissociative Identity Disorder (DID).

I knew a woman with this disorder who was successfully treated with Fabian Therapy. She had five distinct personalities – a bisexual sex worker, a violent Illuminati enforcer, a Satanic Ritual priestess, a personality for managing all these other *sub-personalities* and there was also the *primary personality*. Each one of these personalities had a different name. Her primary personality was the one she assumed most of the time. Her core personality had been destroyed in her childhood through ritual abuse. Her primary personality was a constructed one that was designed to conceal her other personalities from Christian society. Through her primary personality, she fulfilled her role in life as an ordinary wife, mom, and part-time worker at a mundane job. Her primary personality was a Christian who had no awareness of her *alter-ego personality* as a Satanic priestess. Her brother, who was in the Illuminati, purchased her back from another Illuminati member and turned her over to Fabian therapists. These therapists no longer allowed her sub-personalities to be triggered and worked only with her primary personality. After a long period in therapy she was able to recover enough of her memories so that she could no longer be triggered or controlled by anyone.

However, in the course of her treatment her primary personality was systematically transformed. As her sub-personalities became inactive, her primary personality began to take on some of the traits of these sub-personalities. For example, one sub-personality had been trained to fire a handgun and use techniques of karate. One day, to her surprise and the surprise of her husband, the primary personality discovered that she was an skilled marksman and martial arts expert. The story she told me was that her husband took her to a firing range to give her some basic self-defense training and was shocked when it turned out that she knew more than him. Another change in her personality had to do with her religious beliefs. Her primary personality had been a very narrow-minded Christian with intolerant views of other faiths. But as her Satanic priestess personality memories became integrated into her primary personality, she became more open-minded in her beliefs and spiritual practices. Another thing that she had to deal with as she recovered from MPD was her feeling of guilt. Under the influence of

Illuminati mind control she had been forced to do things which went against the values of her primary personality. This woman was a success story for Fabian Therapy; she was able to disconnect from the Illuminati and live a normal life. However, I know that she never completely got over all the deep emotional scars created from her abuse.

Although she was someone who suffered from MPD, not all persons who are subjected to Illuminati mind control have multiple personalities. Sometimes less extreme forms of mind control are used to make small adjustments in the personality of someone who's creating problems for the Illuminati. For example, earlier in this book I tell the story of a reporter who was going to expose the truth about the Illuminati. However, before he could do that, he was given a knockout drug in a drink at a bar then taken to a house where he was given suggestions in a structured way. This was done so that he would automatically dismiss anything he heard about the Illuminati as a conspiracy theory. He was given implanted commands so that he would not be able to remember having been programmed. He didn't develop multiple personalities, but he did drop his story and never investigated the Illuminati again. Many persons in our contemporary society have been "adjusted" in this way to make them conform to the Illuminati plans in some way. Such persons usually don't have any idea that they've been tampered with.

A Visit to a Luciferian Temple

I think it might be useful to understand how mind control is abused by those who understand it. This culture of mind control is very well organized and is very well funded. Many of the mind control experts have sadistic personalities. These are persons who take pleasure in humiliating others. In order to free yourself from the grips of such persons, you must see them for the depraved persons they really are.

Consider the saying, "All power corrupts, and absolute power corrupts absolutely."

There is a personal story from when I was thirteen years old that I can tell you which demonstrates this. The Baron needed a favor from an powerful man in another city. So I was taken on a four-day trip. Basically I was supposed to sexually service this man in exchange for a business favor that was to be done for the Baron. And the Baron was going to do a business favor for my clueless nuclear family. In some Luciferian secret societies, pedophiliac sex is a kind of currency. Although in my case, because of my age, this was really hebephilia, which is an attraction for children that are in early puberty. This comes from a Greek root word for youthful beauty. Generally it involves children between 11 to 14 years old.

I wasn't allowed to know what city we were going to. We rode there in a Winnebago Minnie Winnie. I stayed in the back during almost the entire trip. Two other men, Bob and one of the Baron's servants drove the vehicle and stayed in motels at night. For some reason the Baron refused to let me bring any boy's clothing and at thirteen I didn't really pass as a girl so easily anymore. My voice was changing and I was getting taller and my shoulders wider. So I spent most of the trip hiding in the back of the little Winnebago in my girl's clothing. I killed time by reading Nancy Drew detective stories which had been left there by Bob's sister.

I had been told that I was going to visit a Luciferian temple and do some sex work for a powerful man who was a fan of the child pornography films and photos that had been made of me. I didn't like doing this type of sex work but by that age I was resigned to it.

When we reached the temple, the Winnie was pulled inside into a large garage area that was underneath it. We went up an elevator to an upper floor. The building was very upscale. There were beautiful painting on the walls and expensive statues.

I had been trained to act in a very specific way when dressed up like a girl. Everything was programmed, my facial expressions, my posture, how I walked and how I talked. I was dressed up like a doll, and I was to act like a feminized robot who happened to be a boy. I didn't really look like a girl, and I don't think that I was all that attractive. I think what turned them on sexually was that I acted robotically. These people were obsessed with control.

We went up to a mid-sized lecture hall that had a small stage area on one end. There were men in there who all wore masks, and they were all in business suits. There was a woman wearing a decorative, full-face silver mask who sat at the back of the hall with several other people. She sat on a chair that was raised higher than everyone else, and she had a silver crown on her head. I can't be certain whether she actually was a woman or a man dressed in drag.

This was a type of mind-control demonstration. I was the first act. Pornographic pictures of me that had been taken at various time in my childhood had been passed around to the men in the audience, many of whom sneered with lust as they looked at them. I got up on the stage and performed a striptease then sexually serviced a man. I acted out my part very robotically, but from my point of view, that was just part of the act. I wasn't really an unfeeling robot. I felt embarrassed and ashamed, and when it was over I felt relieved. Then I dressed and sat down in the audience next to Bob and the Baron's servant.

In the next part of the demonstration, the speaker, who was some type of mind-control expert, took out a plate that had human feces on it. He walked around the crowd and let everyone look at the plate of feces up close. I remember that there were little bits of partially digested pieces of corn in it. It stank like feces. There could be no question as to what it was. Then he went up on the stage and put it on a table that had two chairs on either side. And there was silverware on the table. He brought in two middle-aged women who seemed to be under his control. He made suggestions to them that they had not eaten anything in days and that on their plates was the most delicious chile ever made. He told them that they could eat all they wanted. The two women started eating the feces as if it was delicious food. The men in the audience laughed at this display. Then he told the women that they were alone in the desert and that it was so hot that they had to take their clothes off or they would pass out from the heat. So they stripped. The controller put another bowl on the table. Then he told them that they were sunburnt all over, but in the bowl was suntan lotion that would heal them. But in the bowl there was really cow manure, which he had also shown to the audience earlier. The women covered themselves systematically with manure as the audience laughed. These women were lead away to a shower room somewhere, while they were still in a trance state.

The final act was a man who looked like he was homeless. He was in a trance state also, or under some type of mind control. He was told that there were leaches on his arm and that the only way to get them off was to burn them off with a cigarette. He was compelled to burn himself repeatedly with the lit cigarette while the audience laughed. After he was lead away, the speaker explained various methods of mind control, and how ultimately they would be used to control the entire population.

Later that day when we left the building through the garage area in the Minnie Winnie, I looked out through the curtained window, although I wasn't supposed to. I saw that the building was some type of Freemasonic building. I don't know what city we were in.

The Social Impact of Mind Control

The victims of MK Ultra and Monarch Mind Control often do not understand that they have been programmed. It's difficult to estimate how many Americans have been subjected to some type of Illuminati mind control, but we are talking about many thousands of people, most of whom have no idea that they have been programmed. Important Freemasons, military personnel, government officials and corporate leaders are often subjected to Illuminati mind control with *implanted* (or *embedded*) commands. Key persons throughout society have been subjected to Illuminati mind control, and most of them do not realize that latent mind control commands have been installed.

The Illuminati have many methods for doing this. For example, I know that certain dentists have been recruited by the Illuminati, and when they put a client under general anesthesia, they implant commands into the victim's subconscious mind. Another practice is that wealthy Illuminati members have large parties where drugs and alcohol are used. At such parties it's easy to put knockout drugs in someone's drink, then have that person taken off to a room where commands are implanted. One way billionaire Illuminati members ensure the loyalty of those who work for them is through implanted mind-control commands.

The Illuminati controls the mass media: the press, television and movies. Illuminati leaders use these mass media outlets to present visual symbolic triggers to the public. These symbolic triggers stimulate implanted commands. Some of these symbolic triggers are images of monarch butterflies, teddy bears, the single eye, the pyramid, the pentagram, the mask, the maze, the goat's head, and many others. These Illuminati symbols reinforce the implanted commands and keep the victims in line. Anyone who feels lightheaded when staring at any of these symbols may have been subjected to Illuminati mind control.

What has happened in America, Israel and Europe is that brainwashing on a massive scale has taken place. Society is being structured by brainwashing specialists who don't inform the victims that they have been brainwashed. **Unless you have a great deal of knowledge about how mind control works, you may have been programmed against your will and without your knowledge.**

Anyone who has noticed that they have unexplained periods of missing time in their life may be a Monarch mind-control slave. Even if you've never been subjected to trauma-based mind control, you probably know someone who has been. That's how widespread this is. There are varying degrees to which Illuminati mind-control victims have been affected. However, the mechanism through which all such mind control operates is *memory*.

Memory

Memory is at the heart of mind control. What trauma-based mind control does is to attack the memory system. To heal the memory system you must understand its nature.

There are different types of memory. The terminology I am going to use is as follows:

Memory is any mental record of an experience or of information; it is also the ability to retrieve these mental records. Memory is experienced subjectively in the mind. It may consist of words, symbols or images.

Long-term memory stores, manages and retrieves information or experiences. This memory may last for days or years. This is contrasted to *short-term memory* which is the *working memory* that you use to decide whether or not you want to memorize something.

For example, while listening to a lecture, your working memory will be evaluating the information presented and you would decide what information you should forget, and what facts to memorize for a test. That's working memory. And the stuff you choose to forget is *short-term memory*. The information that you choose to memorize becomes the *explicit memory* that you deliberately select for memorization.

Then there is *subconscious memory* and *conscious memory*. Memories you can recall are conscious, and memories that you can't recall are subconscious.

Your mind is always recording new memories whether you are conscious or unconscious. Even if you are drugged to a state of unconsciousness, everything you hear or experience during that time is recorded by the subconscious mind. And, under exactly the right conditions, carefully worded verbal commands contained in the subconscious memories can direct your thoughts and behavior. This is what the psychic driving of MK Ultra was trying to do – to program the subconscious mind with recorded messages while the victim was drugged unconscious. The MK Ultra techniques used by the psychiatrist Donald Ewen Cameron tended to be unsuccessful at this. But later Illuminati brainwashing research was able to develop techniques for reliably creating these types of subconscious memories. So in spite of Cameron's failure, other successful techniques for psychic driving have been developed. These psychic driving techniques create a type of memory that can be used to control the victim.

I refer to such memories as *occluded memories* because they have been deliberately blocked from the conscious mind. Occluded memories contain implanted commands. *Implanted commands* are instructions made to a slave by an Illuminati controller. They are called implanted commands because they are placed methodically within a unit of memory that has been blocked. The blocking of the slave's memory is caused intentionally with trauma, pain or drugged unconsciousness.

In ordinary life, an individual may repress a memory if it contains overwhelming pain or negative emotions. *Repressed memories* are also subconscious so a child who witnesses his father beating his mother and represses the memory, may grow up to batter his own wife. However, while in therapy he might remember his repressed memory and change his behavior as a result. Such repressed memories differ from occluded memories in that the repressed memories aren't intentionally created, but they come about as an accident of life. Nonetheless, repressed memories can lead to mental illness, and sometimes they can be treated successfully with the techniques of common psychology.

Both occluded memories and repressed memories are toxic memories which exist in the subconscious mind. In both cases they undermine the individual's ability to think rationally and express his or her free will. The therapeutic removal of toxic, subconscious memories is essential to mental health.

But not all memory contained in the subconscious is toxic. Many pleasant childhood memories are subconscious. Such memories haven't always been repressed – sometimes they've just been forgotten with time – but they are always there, in the subconscious. Most of our subconscious memories are benign.

Conscious memories are of two types – *semantic* and *episodic*. *Semantic memories* consist of information that you've consciously memorized. This would be information such as your phone number or facts of history that you learned in school. Semantic memories are made up of words or symbols. *Episodic memories* consist of your experiences in life – specific events, like walking in the park or playing in a baseball game – these are real events that take place in your waking life. Episodic memories are made up of recalled images, sounds, smells, tastes and feelings. Episodic memories are like movies in your mind containing full sensations and perceptions.

Then there are the memories of purely subjective events such as *dream memory*. This is your ability to recall some of your sleep dreams. Also there is the memory of imagination. For example if you were to close your eyes and daydream that you are sailing on a yacht – then later on when you remember this daydream – that would be *imagination memory*.

Confabulation is when imagination memory gets tangled up with or confused with episodic memory. For example if a hypnotist were to make a posthypnotic suggestion that you were abducted by a UFO, and after you were awakened you had memories of the imaginary abduction, that would be an example of confabulation.

Illuminati mind controllers use deliberate confabulation to confuse the minds of their victims. For example, if a man were to be drugged unconscious and then was raped by an Illuminati controller, a suggestion might be made so that he remembers the experience as a UFO abduction where he was anally probed. All the humiliating emotions and painful sensations of the memory would be real; only the context of the experience would be altered in the victim's mind through hypnotic suggestion. So a person recalling a confabulation of what he thinks is a UFO abduction might really be recalling Illuminati sexual abuse. I should point out that in saying this, I am not trying to be humorous, because there really is nothing funny about this.

But I am using this only as an example. Although some people do have false memories of UFO abductions implanted into their minds, I do also believe that some persons actually have been abducted by hostile aliens. And I believe that Fabian Memory Techniques can be used to help such persons. (See page 161 – Fabian Therapy for Helping Abductees.)

Addressing Memory in Therapy

In conventional "talk therapy", the therapist might try to tease out a repressed memory so it can be analyzed in a session. But this doesn't work well with the victims of Illuminati mind control. Sometimes the occluded memories can't be reached. Or sometimes they are protected by implanted commands for the mind control slave to commit suicide or attack the therapist under any such circumstances.

Painful memories that have been repressed by a traumatized person can be difficult to reach. A hypnotist, in trying to help a patient, might place his patient into a trance state and make the suggestion that such repressed memories can be reached. With ordinary repressed memories this technique of hypnosis may sometimes work to transform the patient's subconscious memories into conscious memories.

But trying to reveal implanted commands within occluded memories is much more difficult. Sometimes a highly skilled hypnotist may be able to help a victim of Illuminati mind control to restore some memories. But even in careful hypnosis, the implanted commands to block memories, commit suicide or attack the therapist may be triggered.

A hypnotist trying to recover occluded memories from a Monarch mind control victim is like a soldier trying to walk through a mine field without a metal detector.

Fabian Therapy is designed to avoid the triggering of implanted commands. The Fabian therapist is like a bomb defuser. He or she defuses the power of the painful memories before they can do harm to the client.

With a few exceptions, Fabian Therapy only addresses conscious memories – these would be episodic memory, dream memory, imagination memory and semantic memory. Fabian Therapy uses an indirect approach. Except for a few rare exceptions, it never directly confronts repressed memories, occluded memories or any painful memories. And yet, with this indirect approach – it frees the individual from the influence of repressed memories, occluded memories and painful memories.

Fabian Therapy is a highly structured, disciplined approach that requires strong determination, patience and time. To understand why it works, you have to understand the true nature of memory.

The people who developed MK Ultra and Monarch type mind control operated on the idea that human memory is like computer memory. They wanted to program people in the way that they would a computer. They wanted human robots. But the human mind is not a machine mind. The human brain is a living, dynamic organism. The human mind is vastly more sophisticated than the artificial intelligence of computers.

The brain is often defined as the physical, tangible aspect of the mind, and the mind is thought of as the faculty for thought and consciousness. The brain/mind has access to many levels of consciousness. Memories are more than just electrochemical recordings in the brain.

One advanced theory suggests the possibility that memories may be part of an energetic mental field that interacts with the brain and that the memories themselves are not made up of neurons, but are actually made up of stable units of subatomic energy. The neurons would be the physical interface point for the mnemonic energies. In this brain/mind theory, memory would be conceived of as an energy field that interacts with the body through the brain and nervous system. Although this particular brain/mind theory hasn't been generally accepted by mundane scientists, it does give you a different way of conceptualizing memory.

The mind is not completely dependent upon the brain, but it does need the brain in order to interact with the living body. Brain damage does not necessarily get rid of all memory, but it can make memory harder to access. There is a plastic quality to the brain so that even if it is damaged, memories and brain functions may still be restored.

But I don't want to go too far into the scientific theories upon which Fabian Therapy is based. Wealthy Illuminati leaders recruit many of the world's best scientists. However, the Illuminati scientists often withhold important scientific breakthroughs from the general public. The scientists who developed this Fabian system were Illuminati members who had become disillusioned with the Illuminati's leadership and were covertly rebelling against it. These scientists had advanced degrees in neurology, physics and psychology. They also had access to scientific information that mundane scientists don't have. I'm not sure that I ever completely understood all of their theories. But I do understand how their system works because the system itself is fairly simple.

Let me put it this way: you don't have to know everything about how its engine works in order to drive a car – but you do have to know a few things. In the same respect, you don't have to understand the advanced theories of brain/mind to understand how Fabian Therapy works, but you do have to understand a few basic principles.

You have to understand that on the deepest level of mind, all memory is interconnected. Although conscious memory can be compartmentalized with trauma, on the deepest level of the subconscious – all memory remains intact and interconnected to all other memory.

The *memory field* is the entire system of all types of memories – conscious and unconscious. The memory field is a continuum of every type of memory that may influence your mind. And all of these memories are energetically connected to one another on the subatomic level of quantum energy. You don't have to understand advanced physics, but you do have to understand that every memory is connected to every other memory in your memory field. The mechanism of connection is unimportant to know, but the fact of their connection is important.

What this means is that if you work intensively with one area of memory, it automatically influences every other area of memory. So if you intensely work with conscious episodic memories, you subtly bleed off the pain, trauma and unconsciousness contained in the repressed memories and the occluded memories.

Occluded memories and repressed memories contain overwhelming negative emotions. This can be thought of as a powerful negative emotional charge. When you work with any area of memory, it influences all areas of memory. So when you work with conscious memories in a structured and intense way, you slowly release the *negative charge* from the occluded and repressed memories. This is why the indirect approach of Fabian Therapy works. When enough negative charge is released in this way, the implanted commands contained in occluded memories cease to have any power. This then releases the Illuminati slave from the control of his or her "owner".

COMMAND WORDS

Another concept that you must understand is that while the implanted commands are made up of words and pictures, the real meaning of the implanted commands is primarily expressed through words. And words are semantical. So by working with conscious semantical memory – explicit memory – you can subtly release the negative charge of the implanted commands contained in occluded memory.

Certain words are often found in implanted commands. The following list is an example of common command words: obey, control, submit, sex, sexual, identity, comply, forget, remember, owner, master, controller, slave.

The scientists who developed what I call Fabian Therapy did experiments where they took people who had been subjected to Illuminati mind control and hooked them up to a biofeedback machine that measured heart rate and breathing. The experimenters then slowly read out loud from word lists. These word lists were made up of a combination of neutral words as well as command words such as those listed above. For example the word list might go like this: oats, obey, October, odd, offer – and so forth.

In this experiment, when reading the lists out loud to the subject, no special emphasis was placed on the command words. But when the subject, a mind control victim, heard a command word, the biofeedback machine showed a reaction, without his or her conscious awareness that those words were command words.

Therefore it isn't just the occluded memories that are the problem, but also the command words contained in them.

Command words stimulate the slave into action. The slave cannot resist this stimulation because of the pain contained in the occluded memory.

But the power of command words can be deactivated by working with vocabulary in a structured way.

The Process of Fabian Therapy

These ideas may not make complete sense to you unless you work with them in some way. Once I started to work with these techniques, the principles upon which they are based became clear to me.

With all that in mind, this is how the methodology of Fabian Therapy works. There are four basic aspects of Fabian Therapy:

1. First there are a number of *journaling techniques*. These can be done by the patient when alone, but should be reviewed to some extent with the therapist.

2. Second there is EMA, *Episodic Memory Analysis*. This is the systematic analysis of non-occluded episodic memories, which must be done with a therapist. This is a very powerful technique when used repeatedly, over time.

3. Third there are *extroversion techniques*.

4. And finally there are *vocabulary exercises* to influence semantic memory. This process actually releases the negative charge contained in the words themselves which make up the instructions of the implanted commands.

Although there does have to be a therapist to manage this process, I have to say that most of the time the therapist's role in this process is so simple that some of the people I knew years ago who were doing Fabian Therapy did not have a degree in psychology or certification as a therapist. For the most part, a Fabian therapist is more like an exercise coach who motivates the patient and provides some necessary guidance. However, the overall process does need to be managed by a knowledgeable therapist with practiced skill. And at times, some sophisticated therapy methods are required.

On the other hand, the patient receiving Fabian Therapy must be highly motivated. None of the standard Fabian techniques are complex, but two of them require daily attention and all of them require some self-discipline and willpower. The patient has to accept the fact that he or she will have to be in this for the long run to get tangible results.

Any therapist that would use Fabian Therapy would have to have commitment. There is an old saying, "Who rides a tiger does not dismount." This is not a process that you want to start with someone and leave undone. If you begin this with someone, you may be in it for years and ethically you can't abandon any patient. To start this process and abandon it uncompleted might cause the patient to collapse into depression or commit suicide.

How long they need to be in therapy really depends upon how extensively they have been subjected to Illuminati mind control. If they've been subjected to Monarch mind control to the point of having multiple personalities, they could be at this therapy for years. However, if they've just been subjected to one or two session of Illuminati mind control, they might recover fully in a few weeks.

I should also point out that the Fabian therapists I worked with believed that they would eventually find a way to speed up the process of recovery.

Journals

Whether or not you've been subjected to mind control, journaling techniques can be very empowering. This is something that anyone could do to empower their lives and to take greater control over their lives.

I have to say that even without the help of a therapist, a person could work with just these journaling techniques and get positive results. I had therapists when I first started to work with these techniques many years ago, and even after my therapists were killed by the Illuminati, I continued with the journaling techniques. Eventually I was able to pull myself up by my own bootstraps, as we are apt to say in Missouri.

So here is a description of three highly structured journaling techniques:

1. The daily episodic journal
2. The daily dream journal
3. An imagination/cathartic journal (that can be done at any time)

The daily episodic journal

The *daily episodic journal* works like this: every day, towards the end of the day, you make an entry into this journal. It doesn't take long. You always write down these three things in the entry:

- Your full legal name (this would be the name of your primary personality if you have MPD),

- The date,

- And a single episodic memory from that day. Preferably the episode will be something memorable. Perhaps you met an old friend, or saw a pretty bird. It should be a positive memory, not something with negative emotions in it.

The episodic memory should be something you experienced in the real world, not something you saw on TV or the internet; the reason that such are no good for this drill is because recorded images are dislocated in time. If you watch the same TV show at two different time periods, the memory of the show is virtually exactly the same in both memories. So this creates a duplication of a memory in two locations in the memory field. But real life experiences are located only once in the memory field.

To do this drill, simply write down and describe that episodic memory in a way that would make it easy to recall later. Then at the end of each week you review the episodic memories that you've written down for that week. Again, at the end of each month you do a review for that month, picturing in your mind each episodic memory in the order you recorded it. I noticed that when I would do these monthly reviews I would often feel the negative charge being subtly released from my subconscious mind. It made me feel as if I was taking back control of my life and regaining my true self. If you do this journaling technique for at least a year, you can do a review at year's end. This review can feel very empowering.

Anyone who tries to use such journaling techniques should have a commitment of doing them for at least several months because it can take that long before you start to feel tangible results. I should point out that if a person has MPD and they notice that entries are missing on certain days it could indicate that an alter-ego personality had hijacked control during those days.

Some entries made in such a journal might be as follows:

John Smith – Sept 20, 2013 – Took walk in park during lunch break. Saw girl in red dress playing frisbee with man in blue jean jacket. Laughed when I saw their dog steal the frisbee and run away.

John Smith – 9/21/13 – Ate breakfast at cafe and ran into my old friend Jane Jones. We reminisced about our days in college.

John Smith – 9/22/13 – During Sunday Service the children of the Church did an amusing puppet play where they dramatized the six days of creation in Genesis.

The daily dream journal

The *daily dream journal* is also done on a daily basis. For practical reasons you may not always be able to make entries into this on a daily basis. Some nights you might not have dreams, and some mornings you might have to get up in a hurry. But when circumstances allow, what you do is that you simply write down what you remember of your dreams from the night before. In the evening, before going to sleep, put a notebook and pen next to your bed where it can be easily reached.

Not everybody remembers their dreams. But the funny thing is that many people discover that once they start doing the daily episodic memory journal, they start to have nightmares, and these nightmares are usually memorable. It's also true that if the patient is doing EMA on a regular basis it will indirectly stimulate nightmares during sleep. And actually, if you do start to have nightmares, unpleasant as they may be, it's actually a good sign that the therapy is working. It's through these nightmares that the subconscious mind is releasing the negative charge contained in occluded memories.

However, you don't have to analyze the dreams in any way. Just write down the content of the dream – no matter whether it was happy or upsetting. If you dreamt you were flying – write down, "I was flying." If you had a dream you were being chased – write down, "I was chased." Keep it simple.

There are different systems for analyzing dream symbolism. Some of these systems are based on psychology and some are based on mysticism. For our purposes, you don't need to analyze the dreams for symbolic meanings.

By simply paying attention to your dreams and writing them down you eventually come to release negative charge from your memory field. This technique takes advantage of the mind's natural healing processes. Negative emotions and memories that have been repressed from the conscious mind automatically come out in dreams or nightmares. When you make a commitment to write down your dreams on a regular basis, you automatically stimulate this natural mental process.

However, writing down dreams can get to be kind of boring after a while. Because it was helpful, I did dream journaling for years. To keep myself interested in this type of journaling, I got some books on dream symbolism from the library, and when I was doing this type of therapeutic journaling, I would analyze dream symbols just to make the practice more interesting and keep me doing it everyday. But the scientists who developed Fabian Therapy always insisted that such analysis isn't necessary.

Some entries for the dream journal might go as such:

> *Ate lunch at a fast food restaurant on the moon. I decided that the food tasted bad, but the other patrons kept eating.*
>
> *Dreamed I was flying. Slowly arose above the trees and went up into the clouds.*
>
> *Nightmare that I was being chased by demons across a barren landscape. Woke up sweating.*

The imagination/cathartic journal

The *imagination/cathartic journal* does not have to be done every day, but only when you feel like it. Its purpose is to use your imagination to address and release negative emotions. What you're doing with this journal is that you're trying to purge negative feelings. You're not trying to figure out what happened to you. The purpose of this journal isn't investigative, it's cathartic. This journal can consist of written words and drawn pictures.

This journal is for yourself. You don't have to show it to anyone else, though you can share it with someone else if you choose to. But you should only share it only when you feel it's appropriate to do so. Most victims who have been subjected to Illuminati mind control have bad feelings that they carry with them. They don't really know where the feelings come from or why they are there. At times when you have these bad feelings, you can express them on paper with words and pictures. You might find that you sometimes write things or draw pictures that you would feel embarrassed to show somebody else. You should use your own judgement as to whether or not you share with others what you write down or draw. This journal is for you, not anyone else.

The idea here is to express these bad feelings in words and pictures.

There is no right or wrong way to do this. You don't have to have artistic talent. Nothing you write or draw needs to make sense. This process isn't intellectual; it's emotional. This is just another outlet to release negative charge from the memory field.

During the more intense periods of recovery I wrote and drew volumes of materials. I had boxes filled with this stuff. Sometimes I put my musings into the form of fantasy stories to keep myself motivated. Years later when I looked at this material I realized that I had produced nothing of literary value, but the physical process of writing and drawing had been a tangible way for me to release negative emotions.

Eventually I found it cathartic to ritualistically burn up what I had drawn and written about the abuse.

EMA – Episodic Memory Analysis

EMA, Episodic Memory Analysis, is the systematic analysis of non-occluded episodic memories. EMA requires a therapist. Non-occluded episodic memories are conscious memories which do not contain pain or negative emotions. These episodic memories are of happy experiences in life. What the therapist does in this process is to ask a series of questions that help the patient to go into such memories intensely.

In this indirect, Fabian approach to therapy you are indirectly influencing occluded memories by intensely focusing upon happy, non-occluded memories.

Envision the memory field as being like a spider web in which all memories are connected to one another through thin strings. If you poke any area of the web, it will wiggle all the other areas. So if you intensely emerge the consciousness of the patient into one area of memory, it will gently influence all the other memories in the memory field. This is not like mechanical memory such as the memory a computer uses, for computer memory isn't based on consciousness the way that human memory is. What quantum physicists have realized is that consciousness is intrinsic to the universe. What advanced neurologists are beginning to see is that consciousness is the web that holds the memory field together.

The goal of this type of memory analysis is for the patient to re-experience a pleasant memory as fully as possible. The role of the therapist is to use his intellect to guide the process, but the patient should not intellectualize at all. For the patient this process should be as experiential as possible. The client's motto should be: "*Don't think about the memory – experience it.*"

This therapy doesn't require a hypnotic or altered state of mind, so the patient should not close his or her eyes while recalling the memories. I have to emphasize that the patient should not intellectualize the process; for the patient it should be purely experiential. Any memory worked with in EMA should be a happy one which does not contain pain or unconsciousness. It also should not be a memory that he or she has dwelt upon a great deal; that is, it should be a fresh memory that has not been analyzed or talked about very much. To avoid embarrassment, it should not be a sexual or romantic memory. And the memory should be an experience in which drugs or alcohol were not used; that is, a sober experience.

To help you understand this process, I've written down a dialogue below which I have reconstructed from one of my own therapy sessions.

Therapist: *Can you think of an appropriate memory for us to work with today?*

Patient: *I went to a baseball game the other day.*

Therapist: *Great. To the best of your recall, what was the date and time that this episode began.*

Patient: *I happened two days ago, I think from about one until four PM.*

Therapist: *OK. Let's start with your olfactory recall, what smells do you recall?*

Patient: *I remember the smell of popcorn as I was standing in line to get a hot dog. There was the smell of the hot dogs cooking. Let's see. There was the smell of stale beer on the ground near the beer stand. When I went to the rest room I recall that it stank of urine. In the bleachers I was sitting next to a man wearing a heavy aftershave. I recall someone smoking a cigar. The day was pretty hot, I recall the smell of body odor.*

Therapist: *Was this your body odor or someone else's?*

Patient: *Both. And there was something else, I'm not sure what it was. Oh yeah. My friend had sunscreen for his arms and he gave me some.*

Therapist: *What did that smell like?*

Patient: *It had a slightly coconut smell, but mostly it had a chemical smell.*

Therapist: Good. Are there any other recall of smells?

Patient: No.

Therapist: OK, then let's go on to an analysis of your recall of tastes in the episode.

In a systematical manner, each of the different category of perceptions contained in an episodic memory are analyzed in this way. The questions of the therapist are only intended to keep the patient's attention focused upon recalling and experiencing the memory. A session of this type should last from a half hour to forty-five minutes. The patient is not in an altered state. But he or she should be relaxed and comfortable.

When I first started doing this type of therapy, they would encourage me to close my eyes when I recalled the episode, but then later on they changed their attitude about that. They came up with what they called the "Gray Room". They had a large walk-in closet in their therapy house. They cleared out that room and painted it middle gray. Then they put in a middle gray carpet. Then they put in a comfortable chair that was painted middle gray. The room was illuminated with a dim bulb. The therapist would sit to one side of me as I sat in the comfortable chair. So I wasn't face to face with the therapist. So when we would do EMA work, we would sit in the Gray Room and I could recall the memory while my eyes were open. But the space that I was staring at when I recalled the episode was a neutral gray.

Furthermore, the therapist should avoid judging the patient or evaluating the reality of the patient. The mind of the Illuminati mind control victim has been tampered with. Therefore even the ordinary recall of episodic memories might contain distortions. If the therapist hears something that doesn't sound right, he should not question it. For example, if in describing a happy memory of a family picnic the patient were to say something like, "And then Mickey Mouse flew through the air, killing a chicken."

The therapist should not question such a statement even though it doesn't sound rational. In such a case the therapist should just continue on with the process. If a statement seems too disturbing, the therapist ends the session and brings the client fully into the present time. But the therapist never questions a seemingly irrational statement. The therapist doesn't judge the validity of the client's statements made during EMA; he accepts them.

It is also true the the morality of Illuminati mind control victims has been tampered with. The patient might, for example, recall a happy experience where he shoplifted something. The therapist should not pass judgement on the patient's lack of morality in enjoying shoplifting. The rule for the therapist is to not judge or evaluate but to just help the patient keep focused on the experience of recalling a happy memory.

There are a number of different types of perception contained in an episodic memory. The Fabian therapist works through an eight-category list in this order:

1. olfactory (smell)
2. gustatory (taste)
3. tactile (touch)
4. emotions (affectivity)
5. personal movement (subjective kinetics)
6. vision (sight)
7. auditory (sound) and
8. linguistic (language)

Frequently recalled memories have a plastic nature to them. The more you go over memories and talk about them the more likely you are to change them in your mind. But the EMA therapist wants the patient to directly re-experience the memory as much as possible without personal alteration. This is why the list starts off with the recall of smell, taste and touch, because the patient is not likely to evaluate them but to just re-experience them. Analysis of sight, sound and language is left to the end of the session because they are likely to be evaluated and altered by the ego of the patient in memory recall. But if the patient is first directed to a direct experiencing of memory by focusing on things like smell and taste, then he or she will continue with that direct re-experiencing throughout the entire session.

The eight categories are used sequentially and the therapist tries to direct the patient to follow this sequence; that is. you start with category 1, move from there to category 2, etc., ending with category 8. When you complete this last category, the session has ended. However if for some reason the client doesn't exactly follow the intended sequence, the therapist should not make an issue of it, but should just let the client experience the memory freely. The eight categories exist to give the therapist a structured way to ask questions. The questions are asked to encourage the client to directly experience a happy memory. It's the client's experiencing of the memory that matters.

The Fabians believed that this process of EMA actually evokes the creation of endorphins in the brain. Endorphins are peptides (pleasure-causing hormones) that activate the body's opiate receptors, causing an analgesic effect. The Fabians used EMA as a non-drug way to treat depression; this is one reason why Illuminati psychiatrists and big pharma have suppressed public knowledge of this EMA technique.

As much as possible, try not to commingle the different categories of memory perception. For example when analyzing category 7, the audio perception of a memory, the patient would be discouraged from focusing on the meaning contain in a conversation he heard because that is what is analyzed in category 8. In such a case, the therapist would direct the patient back to a pure perception of audio memory by asking how loud or soft the conversation was especially in comparison with other audio perceptions. For example the therapist might ask "How loud was the conversation as compared to the sound of the traffic in the background?"

In category 8, first ask the patient to focus on spoken language, then written language in words and finally symbols. "Symbols" means something that is not a word but which conveys meaning – such as a cross, or a traffic sign warning of deer.

When having the patient concentrate on tactile perceptions (category 3 within an episodic memory), questions would be made up such as "How hot or cold did it feel?" Tactile perceptions involve temperature, pressure, discomfort, comfort, wetness or dryness on skin, fullness or hunger, roughness or smoothness, texture and things like that.

Analysis of vision memory, category 6, would involve things like colors, shapes, patterns, brightness and darkness. It would also include the visual perception of movement, such as the perception of a baseball flying through the air or people milling about in a crowd, but an external type of visual perception of movement should be distinguished from personal movement that is felt within one's own body.

Personal movement or kinetics, category 5, involves the perception of movement physically experienced with the memory. This is both the individual's personal movement and the movement of objects which directly influence the individual. For example if you were in a car you would feel the automobile's movement in your own body as you bounced around. However, if you had recall of walking down the street, there would only be the movement of your body unless somebody else brushed into you. If you were playing touch football with friends, your actions – as well as the motions of the other people – directly influenced you. In this sense, there may be some overlapping of the perceptions in categories 3 and 5. Movement that you personally feel is category 3 or category 5, but a movement that you merely see – such as a bird flying – would be analyzed in category 6. One way to deal with this overlapping in therapy is to not worry about following the categories too exactly. If there is some overlapping, it won't really matter. When you try to get the client to focus on his feelings of touch, he might come up with some visual perceptions. Never criticize the client. Just accept what you are told and move on with the process.

Emotions, category 4, would be both the perception of other people's emotions and the perception of one's own emotions. The patient can know his or her own subjective emotional responses, but can't know the actual subjective experiences of others. To keep the patient from speculating about what other people are experiencing – limit the perception of other people's emotions to describing what emotions are expressed by the other person with facial expression, tone of voice and body language. With such physical indicators, the patient should be able to read basic emotional responses such as anger, disgust, fear, happiness, sadness, boredom, indifference and surprise. Studies have shown that these eight basic emotional responses to life are found in all human cultures and can be easily read through facial expression and body language. So the patient is asked not what other people were actually feeling inside but rather what emotions were communicated through their body language, facial expression and/or voice inflection.

However, the patient's own subjective emotional responses may be more complex. And the patient should be allowed to describe these personal emotional responses in whatever way he or she chooses. So in category 4, the patient's perception of other people's emotions should be objective, focusing on the perceived perception of their emotions as revealed through facial expressions and such; however, the patient's perception of his or her own emotions is subjective. The patient's subjective emotions might be described as melancholy, optimistic, perplexed, conflicted, euphoric, infuriated and so forth. But the description of other people's emotions would be simpler. Things like "He looked angry because his face turned red," or "Her facial expression was one of disgust."

During the analysis of emotions in an episodic memory, there will be an overlapping of perception categories.

Internal feelings can be addressed under emotions as well, things like the feeling of hunger or fullness and feelings of pleasure. Again don't worry about some overlapping.

The final category 8, deals with language and meaning, therefore it is more intellectual. Here the patient would focus on the meaning of any conversation that took place in the memory. Also the patient would focus on his or her recall of any written messages that were read in the memory and the meaning of any symbols recalled in the memory. For example a stop sign would be a symbol that has meaning. Also a cross on a church steeple would have symbolic meaning.

Generally speaking, the episodic memory chosen for this type of analysis should be a happy one. The patient might actually choose to create a happy experience in his or her life to be later used in Episodic Memory Analysis. For example, one time I intentionally went to a baseball game prior to a therapy session so I could analyze it in therapy.

Recent memories that are easy to recall tend to be a good choice, but older memories that are easy to recall will also work. In therapy it's best for the therapist to start out with sessions that address recent happy memories and then after the patient is comfortable with the process, older happy memories can be used in sessions.

As the therapist works more and more with the patient they will want to start working with memories from differing locations on the memory field. That is, they will want to deal with memories that are recent, and memories of the more distant past. In one session you might analyze a happy memory from last week, and in the next session you might analyze a happy memory from two years ago. The EMA process can be applied to any memory which the patient can reasonably recall. The more you use this process, the more you will increase the patient's ability to remember episodes. With practice, the patient may find that he or she can contact memories from early childhood. The ability of the patient to be able to recall such memories should be the guide.

In doing EMA, it's vital that the patient not be doing drugs and alcohol during the weeks or months when EMA therapy is being practiced. It's also important the the patient get a good night's sleep the night before each session. It's also good that the patient avoid drinking caffeinated beverages prior to the session

There are always certain principles that must be followed in any Fabian approach to therapy using episodic memories. One is that all such episodic memories must be happy and without unconsciousness, overwhelming pain, or strong negative emotions.

In this indirect Fabian Therapy process, the negative charge contained in occluded or repressed memories will be subtly but consistently released.

The EMA acts as a catalyst. What happens is that the feelings contained in occluded or repressed memories begin to surface in various ways. They may come out in dreams. They may come out in art work such as drawings. The patient may have the occasional flashback during waking hours. The point of this type of therapy is not to dwell on the negative feelings that surface but to simply allow them to happen and then get on with life by extroverting your attention on present-time events and people.

EMA Past Life Exploration

Most past lives therapy that is being used today focuses upon painful memories from past lives, but I think that this approach is a mistake. I think you get much more benefit from past life exploration if you focus on the happy memories from past lives.

The Fabian therapists that I worked with did some exploration of past lives with their clients. In this type of past life memory analysis, they only dealt with positive memories. They might ask a question such as "Recall a past life experience where you felt good about accomplishing something." Then the client would locate such an experience. Then they would ask, "When was it?" The response to that question might be an exact date, but it might be something subjective like, "During the Civil War era." Whatever the client's response to that question, even if it didn't make sense, would be accepted by the therapist. They would not judge or question anything that the client would say about the past life.

The point of this therapy isn't to have an intellectual comprehension of what happened in a past life but to create a positive emotional experience. The past life experience would be analyzed with EMA as in the previous chapter.

An interesting point of this has to do with language. The clients might recall a past life where they spoke a language they no longer speak. Commonly, clients recalling such past lives will recall the meaning of what was said even if they don't understand the exact words. Apparently the soul which incarnates from life to life retains an understanding of the meaning contained in language even when the present incarnation doesn't understand the language itself anymore. This is because language is really a type of carrier wave which codes and decodes essential information. Information or meaning exists not as words or symbols but as vibrational wave forms in the Universal Mind of God. So meaning itself transcends language.

Persons who did this type of past-life work would discover that conflicts in their present life had arisen from past lives. And they would learn to process those conflicts. The persons who did this type of past-life analysis often would also develop psychic powers as a result.

However in doing past life EMA the Fabian Therapists would make sure that they only contacted episodic memories that had these traits:

- You felt happy about life.
- You were healthy and whole.
- You were sober.
- There was no unconsciousness in the memory.
- You were not in pain.

If a client did come across a past life whereupon he or she contacted a memory containing upset or trauma, the Fabian Therapists would be sure to bring the client into the present time with extroversion techniques.

Extroversion Exercises

Sometimes in this process of Fabian Therapy, recovered memories of painful experiences will suddenly arise into the patient's consciousness. Rather than going into such memories, the patient is encouraged to retreat from them. That's what these extroversion exercises are intended to do. They help the patient to escape from memories from the past which contain pain and to focus on the present time environment where the patient can feel safe.

For example, in one session of Episodic Memory Analysis, we started to go into a memory that I originally thought was a true memory. I started to recall the time that my Nanny, Shotzy, took me to the zoo. But as we went on in the analysis, it turned out to be a *false memory* that had been implanted by Shotzy.

After torturing a cat in front of me, Shotzy used my emotional trauma from that experience to put me into an altered state where suggestions were made to me. It was suggested to me that I not be able to remember the experience of seeing the cat tortured. It was also suggested to me that in place of that experience I should remember going to the zoo with Shotzy. The imaginary zoo trip was described in great detail to me. I received descriptions of all the animals we supposedly saw, the cotton candy I ate and so forth. After this, I was returned to a normal state of mind. Then, as Shotzy drove me home, she talked with me about the imaginary trip to the zoo we had just made – as if we had actually gone to the zoo. She asked me what I thought about the lion who we saw roar at us, and so forth. I felt compelled to go along with this game of hers until I actually started to believe it was true. So by the time I got home, I was describing the trip to the zoo as if it had really happened. Later I would recall it as if it had been one of the happiest of my childhood memories.

Years later, after I had been in Fabian Therapy for a while, during a session of Episodic Memory Analysis, I choose the memory of my childhood trip to the zoo with Shotzy. However, when we started to do the memory analysis, I couldn't remember any smells. So even at the start of the analysis something seemed to be not right. Then I remembered the malodorous smell of a cat's intestines being pulled out. Then I remembered the truth about Shotzy and what she did to me. At that point, the therapist used extroversion techniques to bring me out of the painful memory and back into the present time. Had he not done this, I might have collapsed into my negative memories of being repeatedly tortured as a child, and this could have triggered implanted commands to commit suicide.

When he became aware that we had encountered a false memory that was covering a memory of abuse, he quickly started to use extroversion techniques. He asked me what that present day's date was. He asked me to describe the location of where we were at that present time. He had me look around the therapy room and describe what I saw there. He asked me to walk around the room and touch things – feeling their textures. Then when he was certain I was focused on the present time, we took a walk together and made small talk as we walked along.

All of this activity extroverted my attention away from my painful memories so that I could focus on the present time. As I walked along, I felt more powerful. I could tangibly feel the negative charge being released from me. I remember that on that day my perceptions all seemed clearer, as if a fog had been lifted from me, and I took pleasure in extroverting my attention on my present time perceptions. This is the kind of thing that happens when subconscious memories are converted into conscious memories.

So when practicing EMA, the therapist will always keep the patient's attention on recalling a happy memory, but if a full-blown negative memory of any kind comes up, then the therapist uses extroversion techniques to bring the patient back into the present time.

Any therapist practicing EMA should have good communication skills and emotional intelligence. The therapist should be professional, friendly and supportive – but not overly sympathetic. When working with a person who has been sexually abused and tortured, it might be a temptation to express deep sympathy – but this can be destructive to the process. Empathy is a better attitude than sympathy. The therapist is not a parental figure working with a child. The therapist and patient are adult equals. The good will of the therapist should be expressed in professionalism rather than sympathy.

Furthermore in EMA there may be unexplainable negative reactions. The patient may get angry for no apparent reason. In such a case the therapist should respond by using extroversion techniques to bring the attention of the patient back to the present time. The basic principle here is that all inappropriate negative emotions arise from a dislocation in time. Something in the past made the patient angry and so now he or she may get inappropriately angry with the therapist. In such a case, both the therapist and the patient must understand that they must bring the patient's attention back into the present time and place. Another thing about negative emotions is that they are always based on fear, so it's important for the therapist to help the patient feel safe.

Extroversion exercises are a necessary part of Fabian Therapy. Extroversion can be thought of in two ways:

1. First, it is simply any technique that brings a person into the present time when he or she has gotten stuck into painful memories of the past.

2. Second, it is an attitude of living an extroverted lifestyle. This means the patient should have a goal of being socially extroverted. Being with other persons in safe, social situations keeps the patient from focusing on the past in a negative way.

Furthermore extroversion also means having one's attention focused on activities taking place in the present time. This can be things like taking a walk, working in the garden or doing physical labor.

For the purposes of EMA therapy, extroversion exercises should be thought of as both social extroversion through conversation with the therapist, as well as perceptive extroversion by getting the patient to pay attention to the present environment. During EMA, the therapist is helping the patient to achieve a deep introversion into a happy, conscious memory. But when the process of EMA is over, the therapist must help the patient to extrovert.

A patient who is in Fabian Therapy is encouraged to not get stuck in painful memories as they spontaneously arise during journaling. This is also true of negative memories that arise in Episodic Memory Analysis, in nightmares or daytime flashbacks of trauma. Although it's a good sign that occluded memories come back uninvited in flashbacks, when this does happen, the patient should understand that while in Fabian Therapy it's best to retreat from such memories. If there is a need for some emotional catharsis, the patient can use the cathartic journaling technique to release negative emotions. Or the client can use drumming or art work to cathartically express negative feelings. But after such cathartic expressions, the patient should extrovert his attention and let go of the experience.

If a session of EMA is interrupted with a strong negative reaction that the patient feels the need to express in some way, the patient should be allowed to write down words or draw pictures to whatever extent he or she feels is appropriate. This can be done for cathartic purposes. But the therapist should avoid the temptation to analyze or dwell on the pictures or words. The idea is that once the negative feelings have been released, the patient should refocus on the present moment.

In a sense, what Fabian Therapy does is to heal the entire memory field through therapeutic memory exercises. In this way the individual takes back control of his or her ability to recall memories. There are two aspects to the memory field:

1. the memories themselves and
2. the mental mechanisms which allow memory to be recalled.

Traditional talk therapy attacks the painful memories contained in the memory field, but Fabian Therapy systematically heals the mind's ability to recall memory through indirect processes. In this way, the individual takes back his or her life.

For years I didn't talk about my experiences with Satanic Ritual Abuse, but I continually did journaling and my ability to remember the abuse slowly came back. After decades of work, I can consciously recall everything that I was subjected to. The way I recall a memory of abuse and the memory of normal childhood life are exactly the same. For example, I can recall a time when my little league team won a baseball game. (My team wasn't very good, this only happened once.) I also recall a time when Shotzy sacrificed a rabbit to Ishtar on a white lace altar before a intricate silver pentacle as she insisted to me that the blood of the sacrifice was beautiful. At one time the baseball memory was conscious and the Satanic sacrifice memory was repressed into the subconscious. Now both memories are conscious. But I never addressed the memory of the sacrifice of the rabbit in therapy. It's just that over time, as my memory field healed, that memory slowly emerged into conscious awareness.

When I first began with EMA as a teenager I had some conscious recall of the abuse that was done to me, but I also had periods of missing time and some mental confusion. As a teenager I experimented with the usual drugs of the 60s, and I often drank too much. But during the time period when I was doing EMA therapy I made a commitment to be clean and dry. There was a period of several years where I avoided my usual drinking buddies and lived a sober lifestyle. It was during that time in my life that I did most of my EMA work. Eventually, I was able to recall the implanted commands contained in occluded memories, and in consciously recalling them I became released from them. For example, I remember the implanted commands made to me that I should commit suicide if I ever started to recall the abuse, but in consciously recalling these recovered memories, I don't feel any desire to commit suicide. These implanted commands have been slowly defused.

But there are still some residual negative emotions. In writing my books, for example, some negative emotions are definitely being triggered. Writing down my memories is difficult. But it is also possible. Someone who had not recovered from this type of abuse would not be able to do this.

Many victims of Illuminati mind control question whether or not they've been abused because they have no touchstone in reality. It's tempting for them to think that the abuse was all just some type of fantasy or confabulation. I have certain advantages over many victims of mind control in that I have had feedback from the real world concerning my abuse. When I was young I had persons I knew in the Illuminati who I could talk with about the cult and its abusive practices. Now, many decades later, I have had some contact with Illuminati insiders who I've talked with about these issues.

When I was a child, I had great difficulty even being able to remember the abuse I received. Even after I got to the point where I could remember the abuse, I had great difficulty talking about it. Eventually, after decades of work, I got to a point where I could talk about it, even on a public radio program. I got to the place where I can think about and talk about the abuse because I have put many years of work into the healing of my memory field.

During those years of healing I deliberately avoided going into the painful memories and instead tried to keep my attention extroverted as much as possible. This was a lifestyle choice. I made a point of attending social events and doing volunteer work. I made a point of going on long hikes and doing things outdoors. My attention was not focused upon myself and my personal problems so much as it was focused on other people and the world around me. Illuminati mind control deeply wounds its victims. Fabian Therapy is a method of slowly healing those wounds. During the years that I was healing myself, I managed to live a normal life and I was not under the control of the Illuminati. Extroversion is more than a therapeutic technique, it is an attitude that makes a normal life possible.

Semantical Deactivation Technique

Here the term *semantical* refers to language, words and symbols used in Illuminati mind control. To be *activated* is to be pushed or goaded toward an action. The words and symbols in Illuminati mind control commands drive the victim toward taking an action or repressing an action. Therefore a victim of Illuminati mind control is a slave who can be activated by command words. To semantically *deactivate* the victim of Illuminati mind control is to lessen the power those control words have over him or her.

All the implanted commands used in Illuminati mind control are based upon spoken words – the implanted commands are essentially semantical. However, the spoken words may also be tied to visual symbols and written words. Think about the power of language. A hypnotist can place a person into a trance using words alone. While under hypnosis a person's heart rate may be increased or decreased – by the words of the hypnotist. Other physiological responses can be invoked with words spoken by the hypnotist. Someone may voluntarily submit to hypnosis, but the Illuminati mind control victim has no such choice. He or she is controlled robotically by the words contained in implanted commands. And all such implanted commands contain a negative emotional charge due to the trauma that has been used to implant the commands.

Let's say a woman is programmed with Monarch mind control. She has been programmed with an implanted command that says, "You will sexually service whomever your owner instructs you to."

The words of that command contain negative emotional charge from the trauma-induced mind control. And it is her inability to confront that negative charge that forces her to obey the command. But the negative charge contained in those words can be slowly discharged and neutralized.

Mental Liberation

This is how it's done: three of the key words in the command phrase above are "sexually", "owner" and "instructs". So the Fabian therapist would create three word lists. Each word list would have only one of the keywords from the implanted command in it. So there would be a list, for example, that consisted of the following words: angel, boat, coat, owner, porch, tree, waterfall.

The Fabian therapist would have the patient go through the list and define each word, then make up sentences containing each word. The therapist would draw no special attention to command keywords, but would treat them in the same way as the neutral words which do not stimulate reactions. In doing this, the process would touch the memory field and subtly discharge negative emotions from any occluded memory that contained those command words.

Semantical memory recall is the ability to understand and use words in communication. In a sense, the Illuminati mind control process hijacks the victim's ability to understand and use words so that command phrases can be used to control the victim. However, by having the patient make vocabulary word lists, he or she can slowly reclaim full conscious control of his or her semantical memory recall. The word list exercise strengthens the patient's ability to understand and use words. This changes how the patient relates to all the words and language contained in the memory field. This ultimately opens a greater conscious awareness of all that is within the memory field.

The therapist might not always know what the command keywords are, so he might have to guess. But consider this: there are certain words you always have to use in the construction of any sentence, words like: *the, and, or, of, a, an, in, this, that*.

So by using word lists put together, even with guesswork, you still are likely to discover some command keywords. And by working on any type of word list, you influence the semantical memory recall function. In doing this, you strengthen the mind's ability to remember. One principle of Fabian Therapy is that by increasing the mind's mnemonic abilities you decrease the power of occluded memories. Having a client work on any type of memory-improving exercise helps repair the overall memory system. Having the client learn new words and memorize their meanings helps to give the client control over words. You want the client to have control over words, rather than to be controlled by them. So simply by working with vocabulary in general and having the patient make up sentences with words defined in a dictionary, you actually decrease the power of implanted commands.

A Typical Fabian Therapy Session

In a typical Fabian Therapy session, I would arrive up at the house where we did therapy and the therapists and I would sit across from each other at a table. They would each have a notebook and pen, and I would have some paper and a pen too, in case I wanted to take notes. I would not go into an altered state of consciousness. And normally hypnosis would not be used. The attitude would be of adults meeting together as equals.

The Fabian therapists I worked with operated always in teams. There would be at least two therapists. Some times both of them would be with me, but usually they would go back and forth and take turns being the primary therapist. The sessions would go on for hours, and we would take breaks.

The therapists would first ask me if I had any ongoing concerns in my life that would keep me from focusing my attention upon the therapy. One time I forgot to bring enough change for my return trip home on the bus, and he gave me some change. But more often than not, it would just be issues in my life that I needed to talk through a little with someone; things like me not getting along with one of my girlfriends or something like that. This initial conversation would usually not take very long and was called *the Preliminaries*. (Read more about *the Preliminaries* at the end of this chapter.)

The Preliminaries were a prerequisite to doing *Episodic Memory Analysis*. That way your attention would be on the EMA process and would not be distracted by some present-time problem. However, when I was first in therapy, most of our time was spent in these *Preliminaries*. The point of all this was to make sure that the client was stable enough to go on with the more advanced forms of therapy.

Because the Fabian therapists were dealing with persons with multiple personalities, they would sometimes use *lie detector machines*. Lie detector machines don't detect lies, they detect emotional responses. But that information is valuable in the case of people with multiple personalities or split personalities. One personality doesn't necessary know what the other personality did or experienced. If the therapist asks the primary personality if he's recently been the victim of violence and he says no, but the machine shows an emotional response, this could indicate that the alter personality has been subjected to violence which the primary personality doesn't recall. So the therapist would know to evoke the alter personality and find out what happened. This way the therapist would be able to help the client avoid being the victim of violence in the future. However, the therapist would want to work with the primary personality as much as possible. So evoking an alter personality would only be done in an emergency situation such as the client's life being in danger.

After that we would talk about my *journaling*. Sometimes I would bring along my journals and we would look through them and they would encourage me to continue with my journaling practice.

Then we might do something like *vocabulary work*, that is Semantical Deactivation Technique. We would go over a word list. I would take each word, fully define it with a dictionary and then make up sentences using that word. The therapist would listen to me as I did this. When the list was complete we would take a break for ten to fifteen minutes. And we might do other things. The pattern of the therapy sessions varied some. But these therapy sessions would last for hours and involved a number of different activities.

If we had time, eventually we would go into the *Episodic Memory Analysis*. This would be the heart of the therapy session. We would usually spend from thirty to forty-five minutes on EMA. Because the focus of such episodic memories is on happy events, I would usually be in a positive mood at the end of the session.

At the end of the session, the therapist would make sure that I was grounded in the present. The attitude that I had to assume was to *be here now*; that is, the main focus of my attention should be in the present moment. Often we would go outside and take a walk and make small talk before I took off to go back home.

It was usually during these walks that my therapist and I together would plan when we would next be in session. The frequency of the sessions depended upon what I felt I could deal with emotionally. Commonly we met once a week, every week. Sometimes we met as little as once a month. When therapy first started we met frequently. The therapy sessions tended to make me feel emotionally stabilized. The more sessions I attended, the more grounded I felt. Eventually we started to meet with less frequency.

One important rule was that while I was in therapy I was to avoid talking with anybody else about the therapy. I mostly only talked about the therapy with my therapists. I did occasionally talk with some other patients who had been through this type of therapy. but I never talked with outsiders about it. This was important for two reasons:

1. Fabian Therapy is a rebellion against the Illuminati who don't like it when people rebel against them, and thus are likely to hurt anyone perceived as a threat.

2. Also it's easier to avoid painful memories if you don't talk with other people about the fact that you're in therapy and Fabian Therapy is based on the avoidance of painful memories.

More about *the Preliminaries,* taken from the author's memoirs: *Angelic Defenders & Demonic Abusers:*

The Preliminaries were the issues that had to be addressed before going into the main therapy session... During *the Preliminaries*, Mr. Fabian would ask a series of question from a list. My recall of the questions were that they addressed issues of health and well-being. These would be questions like:

- Did you smoke marijuana at any time during the last two weeks?

- Did you consume alcohol at any time in the last 36 hours?

- Did you have any unpleasant reactions to the last therapy session?

- Have you made any major changes in lifestyle since the last time we met?

- Have you been ill since the last time we met?

- Have you had an episode of emotional distress since the last time we met?

- Have you been the victim of violence since the last time we met?

- Have you committed an act of violence since the last time we met?

- Have you committed any crimes since the last time we met?

- Have you had any social problems since the last time we met?

- Have you had a serious life problem since the last time we met?

- Have you formed any new relationships since the last time we met?

- Do you have any issues that you need to address before we go further into therapy?

When I would answer "yes" to any of those questions, the Fabians would go into a dialogue with me about it. These discussions would take varying amounts of time. The first two therapy sessions that I had with the Fabians, we mostly just dealt with *the Preliminaries*. By the time that I started therapy with the Fabians, I had become a somewhat troubled young man. The years of abuse had taken their toll on me... I was a typical juvenile delinquent. The Fabians felt that they had to help me to stabilize my life before we started the deep therapy techniques. And that's what *the Preliminaries* were for: to help the client deal with real world problems and stabilize.

Advanced EMA Techniques

What I described above is the typical approach to EMA that my therapists were using at that time, and that approach is relatively easy to understand and describe. But they also had some other, more advanced techniques.

In using these advanced EMA techniques they had a diagram that they would make. Imagine a circle divided into eight different sections. This would look sort like a picture of a wheel with eight spokes. Think about the concentric circles such as those that you would see in a tree ring. Now divide those concentric circles into eight equal sections. That is what the diagram looked like.

- The *eight sections* represent the eight categories described before: *olfactory, gustatory, tactile, affectivity, subjective kinetics, visuals, audio* and *language*.

- The *concentric circles* are a representation of the *different time periods* in the patient's life, such as: *prepuberty, puberty, young adult* and so forth.

- The *center circle* is the *subconscious memories* of the patient from the *prenatal period, birth* and *early childhood*.

- The *surrounding circles* are *subsequent time periods* in the life of the patient so that the *outer circle represents the most recent time*.

- The chart could be divided into years and the sections used would depend on how old the client was.

This diagram was a chart of the patient's life that was used as a tool in helping the therapists move the patient's attention to different points in his memory field. So the chart was like a symbolic representation of the holistic memory field.

They would also use a biofeedback machine in these more advanced techniques. The only purpose of it was to make sure that the patient remained calm, deeply relaxed and without internal conflict. Then they would go to different locations on this chart in a random fashion.

The client would recall the memories with his or her eyes open, and this therapy would be done in a room where everything was of a middle gray color and there were no distractors. The therapists would look at the chart, but the client would not be able to see it. The client would concentrate on only the happy memories.

For example, they might ask the patient to recall a recent happy memory. Having done that, they would ask for a single perception of that memory from one of the eight categories. For example: "Recall a smell in that memory."

The patient would recall a smell: "I remember the scent of a flower."

Then they would go to to a different happy memory in a different time location and a different category of perception. Typically, EMA intensely and systematically analyzes a single recalled episode, but advanced EMA is different. Instead of intensely analyzing the memory perceptions from one episode, they would go from episode to episode and pick only one type of memory perception from each episode.

So the patient might recall the smell of a flower when working in the garden two weeks ago, then the taste of corn on the cob from a picnic ten years ago, then the feeling of cool rain coming down on a hot day during a hike three months ago, and so forth.

This would go on for about twenty minutes. I did this a few times toward the end of my therapy work. You needed to already have had a lot of typical EMA work before you could do this. Sometimes we found that I could recall happy sensations from early childhood – memories I thought I had forgotten. My therapists claimed that some of the people they had worked with could recall prenatal memories.

This type of therapy really made you feel good. It tended to leave you feeling uplifted. It also provided a change from the other type of work.

My Fabian therapists believed that this type of advanced EMA could speed up the process of recovery. They had used this method with certain clients in *The Retreat* and in some cases they had achieved an integration of multiple personalities in a matter of weeks.

If the Illuminati hadn't killed my therapists, I think things might have gone better for me in my life. If they had been able to complete their research on their therapy system, I think it would have benefited me and been a substantial contribution to society. I wish that they had been able to openly publish their findings. But I'm hoping that I'm able to reveal enough about their approach so that others who are doing research about Illuminati mind control may gain insight from what I've written here. I feel confident that someday benevolent social scientists will be able to figure out more therapies for effectively deprogramming the victims of trauma-based mind control.

Basic Deprogramming Theory

Just as there are four aspects to the mind control method, there are four aspects to the deprogramming method:

1. awakenment
2. memory recovery
3. authentic self realization
4. emotional sensitization.

1. Awakenment

Awakenment is the experience of an individual realizing that he or she has been brainwashed. This realization doesn't necessarily happen all at once. The individual might wake up a little at a time. This awakenment happens in different ways for different persons. There is an international "Truther" movement in which internet activists are trying to wake people up. Leaders like Alex Jones and David Icke put a great deal of effort into this type of activism. *Awakenment is the first step in deprogramming.*

2. Memory Recovery

For victims of trauma-based mind control, *memory recovery* is very problematic. But it isn't just the victims of trauma-based mind control who struggle with this. Many people suffer from medical birth trauma, the effects of which they do not understand. Men who have been circumcised as children have been tortured, but most do not consciously remember the torture.

Also there is a deep philosophical meaning to memory recovery. As humans, we are powerful spiritual beings. But most humans have forgotten who and what they really are. Reconnecting with your inner spiritual core is a part of memory recovery because you are recalling your true spiritual nature.

MENTAL LIBERATION

But memory recovery also means the rehabilitation of the memory system. The practice of daily journaling is something that can be useful to many persons because it reinforces the health of your memory system.

3. Authentic Self Realization

Authentic Self Realization: It's become a motto of our time for people to say that they are "looking for themselves" – and this really makes sense because the entire culture has been subjected to varying degrees of mind control. In the case of persons suffering from multiple personality disorder this conflict is intense. When you can reject the false masks of persona that have been imposed upon you and find the person behind the mask, you have found yourself. But this is something that can never be done alone. You need to have relationships with persons for whom you feel mutual respect and affection. Such relationships are necessary in order to know who you are, because we humans are social creatures. Of course some relationships are toxic and destructive. Therefore you have to concentrate on those relationships that are positive and life affirming.

4. Emotional Sensitization

Emotional Sensitization: Most mind control involves varying degrees of disassociation, in which your mental processes disconnect from your emotional awareness and physical sensations. We have all been socially conditioned into ignoring the body's messages, but reconnecting to your feelings is essential to recovery. There is no simple way of doing this other than to pay close attention to what you are feeling – pain, tightness, tension, etc. – and to then respond to those bodily sensations, which are also called feelings or emotions, in a way that helps to release them.

For years I used artwork and drumming to connect with my feelings. I'm not a good drummer. I have no talent for drumming, but when I would feel negative feelings in my body, rather than going into the traumatic source of the feelings, I would drum. Sometimes I would drum for hours. I'd try to express the emotions through the drumming. My drumming might start off as slow and soft drum beats to express apathy and depression. The drum beats would become faster as I got into fear and anger. Often, by the time I finished drumming, the beat would be strong, steady and cheerful.

There are other ways to sensitize yourself to your feelings. I've found yoga and Tai Chi type stretching exercises to be useful for this. Support groups and supportive relationships can be helpful as well. But essentially you must have the attitude that an acute awareness of your feelings and emotions is not shameful but important to your recovery.

Many victims of trauma-based mind control become drug addicts or alcoholics. Psychiatrist encourage psychiatric drug use, which can be very harmful in many cases. These drugs disconnect you from your feelings, while you really need to feel these emotions and process them. Negative emotions can be released in a healthy way with talk therapy, journaling or some physical cathartic expression. It's good to get physical when releasing these negative emotions. There have been times when I've gone out to my car, rolled up the windows and screamed for long periods of time. But most of the time I've processed negative feelings with things like art or drumming.

Sexual Templates from Child Abuse

During my childhood, I was sexually abused mostly by men, but sometimes by women. The pedophiliac abuse never felt good. It was always humiliating, sometimes painful and continually frightening. I felt that I had no choice in these abusive sexual encounters with adults. But after I became a teenager I did have a choice in relationships – or I thought I did. While I was in Fabian Therapy, during the preliminary discussions that we had during each session, it slowly became clear that my childhood abuse had become a template for my sexual behavior as a teenager and in my early twenties. I would have sexual encounters with men, and sometimes women, that were in some ways similar to my childhood abuse.

In my teenage years and during my twenties I generally had a girlfriend with whom I had a normal and usually meaningful relationship. This relationship would be openly known about and it tended to be typical for our age group. These relationships lasted for varying periods of time, as little as a few weeks or in some cases as long as a year. These relationships involved some degree of commitment, and they were emotionally supportive relationships that were usually fun and meaningful.

However I also had brief sexual encounters with men and sometimes women. These were secretive relationships that were short-lived and meaningless. Usually these sexual encounters would involve alcohol or drugs. Most of these were not even one-night stands. These sexual interactions would last a few hours or in some cases perhaps only twenty minutes or so. They tended to be encounters that I felt bad about afterwards. They were less sexually satisfying than masturbation. Sometimes they were dangerous. As a child I had been trained to always use condoms, and that was the case for these encounters. But if I hadn't been trained to be so disciplined in the use of condoms I probably would have gotten a sexual transmitted disease, which I never did.

In therapy I eventually realized that I was having sex like this as an acting out of my childhood abuse. A psychological template for bad sexual encounters had been etched into my psyche through my childhood abuse.

Once I was able to make this connection, I stopped this type of sexual behavior. And I did go through a long period in my life where I became celibate because it was less confusing to just not have sex. I worked on my recovery and developed a deeper sense of spirituality. Eventually I did have a relationship with a woman that lasted for years and was mutually supportive and emotionally intimate. But it took years of healing work to get to the point where that felt normal.

This is something that any person recovering from childhood sexual abuse needs to consider. As a prepubescent child, there is no real pleasure from the sex act. There may be some psychological satisfaction such as being the center of attention or pleasing an adult in a position of authority. But the sex act is really for the benefit of the adult and not the child. But as an adult, when the sex act does have the potential to be pleasurable, behaviors learned in childhood abuse may arise in adult sexual behavior. These patterns of sexual behavior are almost always destructive and ultimately undesirable. You'll know that you've healed childhood abuse when you can release the template for sexual behavior that was imposed upon you as a child.

EMA to Reinforce Healthy Behavior

The Fabian therapists did not have any desire to shape my sexual orientation to either gay or heterosexual, but they were concerned that my choices were healthy. During my late teenage years and my early twenties I acted out bisexually. I do believe in gay rights and I do believe that some people are gay or bisexual by nature. But I also believe that homosexuality was imposed upon me by Illuminati mind control, and for me gay behavior was never a good thing. In other words, I'm not really bisexual, I was acting out that way because of the abuse. And the abuse experience was a toxic sexual template.

Throughout the therapy process, it eventually became obvious to me that certain relationships were healthy and others were unhealthy. A few of my gay interactions were more or less healthy. But virtually every gay encounter was something that made me feel bad afterwards, and often they were dangerous. Some of my interactions with women were equally unhealthy. But most of my romantic and sexual interactions with women were healthy and mutually supportive. The sexual relationships that left me feeling good tended to be with women. The Fabian therapists didn't try to criticize my gay relationships. They did not try to use behavioral techniques to punish gay relationships and to reward relationships with women. Instead the used EMA to focus on my happy memories of romantic experiences with young women.

The Fabian therapists did not ever use EMA to focus in on sexual experiences, even sexual experiences that were happy because they didn't want their clients to become sexually aroused in therapy. But they would focus on romantic experiences that didn't result in sexual activity.

For example, one EMA experience was a high school dance that I took a girl to. We never dated before this or afterwards. And to be honest, I think she was trying to get another boy jealous so that he would date her. There was a boy who had dated her a few times, but then he asked someone else to the dance. So the girl hinted that she wanted me to ask her. I had spoken with her a few times, but she was more popular than I was, and I was surprised that she showed interest in me. I nervously asked her to go to the dance with me while we were on lunch break. She agreed. The dance was a pleasant experience for both of us. But the boy she really wanted to date was there also. He saw us together and got jealous. After the dance he started to date her exclusively. Although there was no sexual content to the EMA analysis of that experience, it was a happy experience for which I had no regrets and only good feelings.

By using EMA to focus on those types of happy dating experiences with women, my behavior did shift. I stopped being drawn to unhealthy sexual interactions and became more focused on healthy relationships. Instead of condemning my drug use and drunkenness, the Fabian therapists would use EMA to focus on the times that I enjoyed myself when I was sober. EMA doesn't shape behavior directly. Instead it speaks directly to emotional consciousness. You focus on the time when you genuinely felt happiness and contentment deep within your heart. This causes you to become drawn to the behaviors that make you feel good, rather than the behaviors that make you feel bad. So the Fabian therapists used EMA to indirectly shift my sexual orientation away from toxic gay relationships and toward natural, healthy heterosexual experiences.

Many persons living gay lifestyles are unhappy. This is not true of all gay people, but it is true for many. So overcoming Illuminati mind control may involve an understanding of how the Illuminati is trying to impose homosexuality on persons who are heterosexual by nature.

Some people are by nature gay persons, and this fact should be understood and respected, but the Illuminati has an agenda to promote homosexual behavior to persons who are not gay by nature. This has to do with plans for massive social engineering. Agenda 21, promoted by the United Nations, contains plans to place all persons in human population centers, which will be like large prisons. One reason for this is to segregate the population by gender the way it is done in prisons. Another agenda has to do with limiting population growth. Prisoners, organized into labor crews, will be separated from persons of the complementary gender, thus pregnancy becomes impossible. There is also the matter of psychological manipulation. Prior to puberty, children are attracted to friendships with other children of their own gender. It's also true that children at this age are deferential to adult authority. Enforced homosexuality is a way to use social engineering to impose a childlike state of mind on adults. They want to brainwash the average citizen to be attracted to same-gender relationships and to be submissive to the authority of the government. This will mimic a pre-adult state of mind.

Individual therapy systems can heal a single person, but there needs to be deprogramming also on a larger scale because the Illuminati brainwashes not just individuals, but whole societies.

Concordance

The Illuminati tries to synchronize the mind control commands made to its individual victims with the propaganda slogans presented to the public through the mass media. *Concordance* takes place when the control words contained in mind-control command phrases also are used as propaganda slogans in the mass media. The Illuminati controls the mass media and coordinates command phrases that appear in the mass media with command phrases programmed into slaves during brainwashing sessions.

Consider the propaganda slogan, *"Too big to fail."* This first appeared through mass media into public consciousness in 1984. The slogan means that if a corporation is big enough, the government must guarantee its success because its failure would destroy society. Of course this is not true. The failure of a large and poorly functioning corporation is good for society and makes the economy stronger. This is how actual free market capitalism works. But it's bad for wealthy stockholders who don't want their investments diminished by economic reality. So this propaganda phrase has been used to justify every type of financial scandal imaginable. But it really isn't a rational statement. Large corporations have failed before without destroying the entire economy. In fact, common sense tells us that the failure of a large, incompetent and corrupt corporation is good for the health of the economy. But whenever the phrase, *"Too big to fail,"* is evoked, the politicians respond like Pavlov's dog and give that large corporation whatever it wants. Many key politicians are victims of Monarch mind control and they've been programmed with the implanted command, *"Too big to fail."*

Whenever the mind-controlled politicians hear that command phrase on the television, it evokes a conditioned response. They know then, on a subconscious level, that they must give that corporation whatever it wants. "Too big to fail," is a *concordant* control phrase. It creates concordance between the individual brainwashed victim and the propaganda used to control the general public.

This *"Too big to fail"* justification has been evoked in recent financial political scams, and has resulted in massive debt and an ongoing depression.

Some typical concordant control phrases are: *"war on terror"*, *"war on drugs,"* *"post 9/11 world,"* *"politically correct,"* *"New World Order,"* *"global community,"* *"hidden hand of the market,"* and *"free market"*.

This coordination of an implanted mind-control phrase, along with the mass media propaganda slogans, prevents discordance within the mind of the brainwashed victim. The brainwashed politician must feel that he is part of a greater movement in society. The politician who has been brainwashed will believe that he is in the right by going along with his programming because that programming is also reflected through the mass media.

However, when mind control command phrases are challenged in life, this can cause the mind-control victim to question his programming. This may cause him to feel anxious, but it also has a potential for releasing him from his mind control, at least to some small extent. The more the public challenges the lies told by the Illuminati-controlled mass media, the more discordance takes place in the minds of the brainwashed politicians.

If you were to hook up the average American politician to a biofeedback machine, and slowly read a word list that contained the words "fail," "too" and "big", you would see reactions on the machine whenever any of those three words were read.

I have to point out that in a sense, the entire population of the United States has been subjected to Illuminati mind control. The Illuminati has been taking over the United States a little at a time since before the Civil War. The Illuminati controls the economy of the United States by using the Federal Reserve. Wall Street is a center of Illuminati power. The Federal Government takes its orders from Wall Street and the Bilderberg Group. The consolidation of all mass media corporations into a very few corporations controlled by the Illuminati, has already taken place.

If you get your news from mainstream newspapers or television outlets you are being subjected to Illuminati propaganda. Ever since September 11, 2001, the entire country has been acting out an Illuminati mind-control drama. The extent to which the average American is disconnected from reality is overwhelming.

Whenever a person watches television or spends long periods of time on the internet, that person goes into a subtle, altered state of mind. In this state of relaxation, the individual is less likely to be critical of any information received. When the Illuminati uses brainwashing techniques on politicians and other important leaders, they coordinate their mind control with the propaganda that the general public is being subjected to. This creates a mind-control continuum which consists of both the propaganda control of the public psyche and the Illuminati's brainwashing control of society's leaders.

Those of us who actually tell the truth about what's going on are labeled as "conspiracy theorists". So if you are freed from propaganda and brainwashing, you are actually out of concordance with mainstream society. This is another issue that a person faces in recovering from Illuminati mind control. The more you attain freedom, the more discordance you feel with this society which is based on Illuminati mind control and propaganda. However, if enough people were to become deprogrammed, there would be a tipping point where society in general would awaken to the truth of what the Illuminati is doing.

Nevertheless, my goal in presenting this information at this time isn't political transformation. I simply believe that the information presented here may have some potential to benefit the mental health treatment of individuals.

Deactivating Mind-Control Symbols

There are certain mind-control symbols, visual symbols, that are used to trigger and reinforce Illuminati mind control. Some examples of these are the single eye, the single eye in the triangle, pyramid with the all-seeing eye at the top, the pyramid, the owl, the butterfly, the umbrella, the goat's head, the devil, devil's horns, the skull, the pentacle, the lighting bolt, the teddy bear, the mask, the maze, the doll, the checkerboard pattern of black and white squares, two columns – one white – one black, the torch of Lucifer, a hand holding the torch, the torch bearer, Mickey Mouse, and various hand signals.

All the above symbols are meant to act as triggers to reinforce various mind control techniques. During trauma-based mind control sessions the victim may be forced to look at such symbols and associate them with conditioning.

However the Fabian therapists had a technique for deactivating the power of these symbols. What they did was to create a series of cards some of which contained these Illuminati symbols but most were images or symbols which had no Illuminati association. Some of the cards had religious symbols from various religions. Some cards were corporate logos or images associated with brands of products. Some were of everyday symbols like stop signs. Some were pictures of ordinary everyday objects like a glass of milk or a flower. The cards would be randomized so that they were never in any particular order. The first time they would go through a run of the cards they would do free association. This is sort of like what some therapists do with ink blots. You look at the card and say whatever comes to your mind.

For example when they showed me the teddy bear card for the first time I free associated the word "pain" with the teddy bear. But they would never judge the free association or get hung up on it. They would just move on. And they accepted whatever free association the client came up with.

Mental Liberation

Then in the next run of the cards, you would make up happy nonsense words which had nothing to do with the symbol. For example, you might be shown a picture of a pentagram and you'd respond with the words, "strawberry jam". Of course that might be a subconscious reference to blood. But they wouldn't get hung up on that. The idea of these nonsense words is that they all have a happy meaning. So no matter what symbol you are shown, you make up a happy nonsense word.

This drill would be done periodically. The result of doing this is that you come to realize that you don't have to accept the meaning of a symbol. It can mean anything you want to make it mean. And when you realize that through the practice of this drill, the symbols stop having power over you and you have power over them.

The all-seeing eye doesn't have to mean the power of the Illuminati, it can mean insight, or any other meaning you assign to it. These symbols don't have occultic power unless you accept that power. You can reject the influence of occult power just as you can redefine symbols any way you choose.

One thing that should be mentioned is that in the course of using this technique, the client would often develop headaches, body aches or strange physical sensations. The therapist would encourage the client to communicate when such sensations take place. At that point, the process of looking at cards would end, and the client would be brought back into the present time using extroversion drills. Then, whatever actions necessary to process the negative emotions would take place. Often the Fabians would use breathing exercises to to release stress and increase relaxation.

Other Uses of Fabian Therapy

I know that the scientists who invented this type of therapy didn't use it only with the victims of mind control. Although their therapy techniques were never presented publicly, they did find people who they could quietly help. I heard the story of a Vietnam veteran who had been traumatized by his war experiences. Fabian Therapy was used to help him heal from his painful memories. It has been used to help persons with depression and other types of psychological problems. In some cases, the therapists would start out with a traditional talk-therapy approach and then switch over to using Fabian techniques. In other cases, they started out with Fabian Therapy and then when the person stabilized, they switched over to typical talk therapy. The scientists who invented this approach believed it could be used as a substitute for psychiatric drugs.

And certain aspects of this therapy approach are commonly used. The Fabian therapists drew ideas from mainstream therapists whenever possible. For example, it's not unusual for mundane therapists to encourage patients to use journaling. If they had been allowed to, the scientists who developed Fabian Therapy would have shared some of their insights with mundane psychologists. However before they could do that, the research project that developed Fabian Therapy was shut down by the Committee that rules the Illuminati.

Illuminati Cultural Mind Control

Thus far we've mostly discussed the way that the Illuminati programs individuals, but the Illuminati is also programing the entire world culture, and you along with it. So there are some things to think about in understanding this cultural mind control. One thing is that Hollywood and the music entertainment business is pretty much controlled by the Illuminati. So any movie or TV show you look at has been designed to program your mind. If you are not very aware of what you are looking at and how these entertainment programs are designed, you are accepting Illuminati mind control every time you watch TV. This is also true of music.

One thing you should be aware of is preprogramming. Think of all the zombie movies that are being put out. In them, ordinary citizens are turned into evil creatures who must be killed in order for the surviving humans to escape. This image of a zombie-filled world is a template that is being programmed into your consciousness. Your subconscious mind is being programmed by these images. You are being programmed to see everyone you come across on the street as a potential enemy. But there is something more than that. Preprogramming means that movies are used to prepare you for future events that the Illuminati might impose upon society. There is a military chemical weapon called BZ. Victims of this chemical weapon may act in a zombie-like manner. Some feel that the zombie movies are being designed to preprogram the public for a BZ attack against the general population by the Illuminati. When victims of BZ begin to act in a zombie-like way, you are preprogrammed to kill them instead of trying to help them.

You have to realize that the Illuminati owns and controls the mass media outlets in Europe and the USA. When you get your news from these outlets what you are getting is a clever mixture of facts and propaganda. Local news has to be more accurate because you have ways of directly checking out events in your area. But no major outlet news program can

Mental Liberation

be trusted. You can't trust the news. You can't trust the history books. In order to be free, you have to question everything. This is a difficult discipline to maintain. But one thing that you have to your advantage is that you were born to have a natural ability to recognize the truth when you hear it. When you pay attention to the feelings that you have in your body, they will reveal truth to you and let you know when you are being lied to.

You need to realize that Psychic Driving, that uses occultic psychic powers, is combined with media propaganda to brainwash the population on a massive scale. The Illuminati have a depopulation agenda and they use movies to forward that agenda. Occultic influencing of the collective consciousness of humanity is reinforced with mass propaganda.

Shortly after the Civil War, a famous Freemason, Albert Pike, created a plan for the Illuminati. This was a plan for Three World Wars. And according to his plan, at the end of those wars, the Illuminati would take over the world and brainwash everyone to believe in "the pure doctrine of Lucifer". We find ourselves now in the midst of this world war three.

Movies are used to program the minds of the public to accept and cooperate with the process of the Illuminati apocalypse. There was a film made in 1916 called *The End of the World*. That was just the start of a deluge of cinematic apocalypse films. The compulsion to make such films doesn't come from public demand. People are just as content to go to see happy films and films that project a positive future. So realize that this type of apocalypse visualization is being imposed upon the public consciousness with evil intentions.

This is just a short list of some of the better known films which promote the idea of an impending apocalypse:

Deluge, Things to Come, The Day the Earth Stood Still, On the Beach, Planet of the Apes, A Boy and His Dog, The Terminator, Waterworld, The Day after Tomorrow, This is the End, Mad Max, The Road Warrior, Dr. Strangelove, Invasion of the Body Snatchers, WALL-E, Dawn of the Dead, Children of Men, Fail-Safe, Night of the Living Dead, The Thing, Shaun of the Dead, Twelve Monkeys, Zombieland, 28 Days Later, Hunger Games, War of the Worlds, The World's End, The Matrix, A.I. Artificial Intelligence, Contagion, Testament, The Dead Zone, Dogma,

Judge Dredd, World War Z, Miracle Mile, I am Legend, The Road, and *Soylent Green.*

Understand this: television and movies are designed to be Illuminati propaganda. When you look at TV and movies in an unthinking way, you are allowing yourself to be brainwashed. The act of looking at a movie or TV actually alters your brainwaves so that you go into a state of light relaxation. This is what a hypnotist does when he relaxes a client in order to make hypnotic suggestions. You are better off if you only watch movies that are funny and life affirming. The less you watch television and movies, the more control you have over your own mind.

THE ILLUMINATI POWER STRUCTURE

When I talk about extraterrestrials, people sometimes roll their eyes. And many people who have awakened to the fact that our governments are really being run by secret societies draw the line at an awareness of hostile ETs. However, you have to realize that the general public has been conditioned to deny the existence of intelligent ETs in much the same way that Pavlov's dog was conditioned to salivate whenever he heard a bell ring. So let's go there. You can't really understand the true nature of thought control until you see the controllers for the intelligent insects that they are.

The symbol of the Illuminati is an owl – which is a bird of prey that operates in the darkness – hence a symbol for secret societies in general. The Illuminati rose to power in part by first taking over the Freemasonic lodges in Europe and the USA. The symbol of Freemasonry and aristocratic Luciferianism is the pyramid. The Illuminati has taken over the Freemasons and all other secret societies in the USA, Israel and Europe. So for many, the pyramid has become a symbol for the Illuminati which is itself organized as a hierarchy with all the power at the top. I have been told that the Illuminati is run by a Committee of three hundred people, but really those three hundred are connected to other powerful, wealthy interests. So realistically what we're talking about is a few thousand people who basically rule much of the world. Their control is not absolute, but they are powerful enough – and criminal enough – that if they really feel threatened by someone they might have that person killed. Supposedly, all initiated members of the Illuminati are themselves protected from such punishments, but in reality if they offend the hierarchy, they can be executed. So if an Illuminati member offends anyone who is on the Committee or close to it, there is the possibility of harsh reprisals. The leaders of the Illuminati are very powerful people who are devoid of moral restraints.

The Illuminati is a personification of an otherworldly demonic empire.

Mental Liberation

I personally believe that the Illuminati is something like a hostile alien consciousness. If you want to, you can think of this as a metaphor: evil aliens rule the world. But you might consider the possibility that this is literally true. The way I visualize the Illuminati is that at the top of the pyramid are dispassionate and intellectual gray aliens. They manipulate everyone with their psychic powers. The Illuminati members who I call the High-Adepts are interested in psychic abilities, but they don't indulge in the sexual rituals or the blood rituals. They are only interested in psychic connections with demons, Lucifer or Satan. I would say that these High-Adepts make up the ruling 1% of the Illuminati. They are the real leaders, but you never see them on TV or the internet. They have a group of criminal enforcers who are loyal to them. These enforcers are Satanists who are obsessed with sex and violence. Some of them have extreme practices such as animal sacrifice, human sacrifice, cannibalism and blood drinking. They make up perhaps 15% of the Illuminati. The other 84% are basically puppets. Some of the puppets may seem powerful – the presidents of the USA and such – but they are just puppets manipulated by the High-Adepts. If the puppets get out of line, the enforcers put them back in line or kill them. And High Adepts have complete control over the enforcers. These High-Adept Illuminati members are gray aliens, or they are possessed by the demonic souls of gray aliens. The criminal enforcers are Reptilian aliens, or they are possessed by the demonic souls of Reptilian aliens. However you look at this, the leaders of the Illuminati aren't really human.

The Sci-Fi movies always describe alien invasions as being fought with spaceships and such, but I don't think this is the case. These aliens are using their psychic powers to invade our planet. The High-Adepts are genteel in their mannerisms. But if somebody crosses them, they have their violent enforcers who can step in.

The Suppression of Fabian Therapy

Back in the early 1980s, the Fabian therapists who had helped me and others got in trouble with the Illuminati. The Committee which runs the Illuminati did not initially object to the idea of a therapy system being developed to undo the damage caused by MK Ultra mind control. Every now and then, after they destroyed somebody's mind, they wanted to restore it again.

I heard a story once of an important scientist whose mind was ruined with trauma-based mind control to the point where he couldn't work anymore. Fearful that he might reveal the technological data that he had discovered, they tried to erase part of his memory and then put him to work on a different project. But the trauma-based mind control wrecked his mental stability, and he wasn't able to work effectively. So they used these Fabian techniques, which I've just described, to restore his sanity and he was able to go back to work for them.

However, the Fabian therapists who helped me also helped many others. They started helping too many people whom they hadn't been authorized to help. And some paranoid members of the Committee felt threatened by their deceptions and disobedience. That is why my therapists were killed.

I had two main therapists. They were a husband and wife team. They were two of the scientists that had developed the basic theories and protocols of what I call *Fabian Therapy*. I also knew of some other therapists who worked at a compound known as *The Retreat*. This was an isolated environment where therapy could be conducted intensively.

I did have a split personality when I was a child and certain events caused my personality to spontaneously reintegrate. But my personality has always been somewhat split. Instead of developing multiple personalities, I had one very complex and conflicted personality. I always could remember some of the abuse, but there were originally some gaps in my memory. Sometimes I had periods of missing time in my life when I seemed to spontaneously disassociate. This usually happened when I was very upset. I was not very functional when I was a teenager. I struggled with life and felt suicidal until I was well into my twenties.

However, I managed to eventually stabilize my life. Part of this was from this type of therapy I received, and part of this was that I had become more spiritual. Prayer and meditation became important parts of my life. But in truth I have never completely gotten over the emotional scars caused by the Satanic Ritual Abuse which I had experienced when I was a child. Emotional wellbeing is something I've struggled throughout my life. I feel disturbed by the knowledge of all the evil things which the Illuminati are still doing to our world. However, I still consider myself fortunate when compared to what I've seen happen to other victims.

Anyone who joins the Illuminati makes an oath of secrecy so that they can't talk publicly about the Illuminati. But I never joined and never took the oath of secrecy. So I am not breaking any rules by talking about this information.

The members of the Committee don't really trust one another – and for good reason. Most of them achieve and maintain power through betrayal.

Some of them would like to see the Illuminati become less powerful and more decentralized. Their motivation in wanting decentralization isn't out of kindness but out of a desire for personal survival. The power struggles within this group are difficult for outsiders to understand. My perception of this situation is that some people on the Committee want this information about Fabian Therapy to be made public, but others don't. I'm not friends with anyone in the Illuminati, but I do have some feeling for how they operate. There are those within the overall Illuminati organization who recognize that the Illuminati must someday be deconstructed and that one element of that deconstruction is the development of therapy systems for treating the victims of trauma-based mind control. So there are those even in the Committee who wish the suppression of Fabian Therapy to end.

Even those persons who are helped with Fabian Therapy still experience problems. The scars of this type of mind control are very deep. And such scars do not heal quickly. Just because you can remember something that you had forgotten due to trauma does not mean that you have healed emotionally. This is why the Fabian therapists were more concerned with creating positive experiences in the lives of their clients than they were with restoring memory loss. The goal of Fabian Therapy is not to restore lost memories, however as the mind is rehabilitated the ability to recall what was once lost memories does take place. So with enough healing you do find that you can remember everything. The goal of this therapy is to free victims of Illuminati control so they are able to function in life. The goal of Fabian Therapy is to help unhappy people find real happiness and contentment again.

I can't say that I've ever been able to completely recover from all the psychological scars of my own experiences, but I can function in life well enough to be able to speak out against the Illuminati – and that makes me better off than most Illuminati mind-control victims. I was well along with my therapy when my therapists were killed, so I was able to continue on with it by using journaling techniques after their deaths. I took the attitude that I could best honor their sacrifice by continuing to heal myself.

I won't go too much into the details of their deaths right now, but I mention this because it points out the problems you might have in trying to help people who are the victims of Illuminati mind control. The Illuminati mind controllers don't want their slaves to be freed. Many victims of Illuminati mind control don't consciously know that they've been programmed. However, the Illuminati's control over their slaves is not absolute. There are slaves who have been highly programmed and who are monitored on a regular basis; such victims would probably be very difficult to help. However, there are a great many people who have only been subjected to a few session of Illuminati mind control, and some of those victims may suspect that their minds have been tampered with. There are always some persons who can be helped, and the point is to help those people who can be.

In a sense the ultimate goal of Fabian Therapy is to heal the world. That is, to create a world where everyone can find happiness in a life of contentment. Many people around the world strive to create such a world, but they are often suppressed. However, someday that suppression will end.

As people become more aware of what is going on with the institutions that have been influenced by the Illuminati, I believe that there will be a movement to eliminate psychiatry. Also I believe that there will be a movement to reform medical institutions and psychology. I believe that my experiences with the Fabians helped to give me a vision of what this reformed psychology will look like.

Institutionalized & Medicalized Mind Control

When I was young I knew that highly-organized Satanic secret societies existed among the wealthy. I knew that they hurt children and were criminally violent. I also knew that if I talked about this publicly, nobody would believe me. But what I didn't understand until I became older was how the oppression of Luciferian mind control is found in the institutions of society. It really is integrated into every major institution.

So you need to understand that mind-control methods aren't just being used by Satanic cults, they are being used by all the major institutions in society. My personal awakening to this fact came about in this way:

When GMO tomatoes first came out I started to eat them, believing that they were safe. The government approved of them and the news media said they were safe. Shortly after this I started to develop a very serious stomach problem. I didn't associate it with the GMO tomatoes, I didn't know what was causing it. But it felt as if I was being poisoned. I experienced intense pain in my stomach, and sometimes the pain was so overwhelming that the only way I could lessen it was to stick my finger in my mouth and vomit. I went to the doctors and they asked what I had been eating. I told them about everything I ate, including the GMO tomatoes, and they eliminated food as the cause of the problem. Then the doctors did expensive test after expensive test. These tests were an extreme financial burden. One of the tests injured me for life and its damage can't be undone. While I was in the hospital recovering from the botched and unnecessary test, they fed me a meal that had GMO tomatoes in it, and this meal made me extremely ill. I was in overwhelming pain for hours.

The doctors never figured out what was causing the problem. But one doctor who was a respected expert did tell me something interesting. He said that my health problem wasn't psychosomatic; it wasn't "all in my head." He knew this because many other people had the same problem and nobody in the healthcare industry seemed to know what was causing it. After months of intense pain and losing thousands of dollars, I gave up on hospitals and doctors.

I finally went to a group of professional psychics that I had heard about. They did a psychic reading where they consulted a spirit guide. The advice that came back was that I should stop eating GMO foods. They also recommended an organic herbal tea that would soothe my stomach. I took the psychics' advice and immediately got better. The psychics did charge a small amount for the health reading, but it was a tiny fraction of what I had paid to the hospitals and doctors who had not helped me at all. I had always been told that people who claim to have psychic ability are quacks and that we should only trust the advice of doctors, journalists and the government. My going to the psychics had been an act of desperation.

And what I realized from this was that some psychics are legitimate and that the fraudulent institutions of healthcare, mass media and government are not to be trusted.

Although I did know about the existence of organized Satanism when I was young, I did not comprehend how it had taken control of so many organizations in society. But I have done a great deal of research since then. Brainwashed puppets of the Luciferian secret societies hold positions at the top of every major institution. Psychiatric institutions are designed to drive people insane. The Federal Reserve is designed to create widespread poverty and financial deprivation for the masses. News agencies disseminate propaganda. The educational institutions limit intelligence and teach falsehoods. The court system imposes injustice on the people. And the hospitals do sometimes cure people, but they also sometimes make people ill.

Psychiatry seems to be particularly toxic. Psychiatric drugs are very destructive. I don't deny that psychiatrists do sometimes help people and that certain psychiatric drugs under certain circumstances can be helpful. But the way that psychiatry is being used today has nothing to do with promoting mental health. Psychiatry has become an institution of toxic social control. And although many people do not realize this, Monarch mind control is being routinely administered in hospital settings by psychiatrists.

Even the way that the Fabian therapists dealt with alcoholism was different than Alcoholics Anonymous. Although I know that AA has helped some addicts very much, there are some toxic ideas in it that make its approach ineffective. For one thing the recovering addict is told over and over that he must accept the fact that he is "powerless". It's nice that AA encourages one to look for a spiritual Higher Power, but to dwell on powerlessness is not healthy. The fact is that we are amazingly powerful beings who have yet to tap into our latent powers. Another thing about AA is that right at the start of their program, they have you dwell on every mistake you've even made in life. All of this is just more brainwashing. It is depatterning and tabula rasa to erase your old personality, then they use *The Big Book of Alcoholics Anonymous* and meetings as psychic driving to create a new personality.

When I was young, I had some very serious issues with drugs. There was a period when I was taking amphetamines and barbiturates as well as drinking alcohol in a way that was very dangerous. This was all a reaction to my childhood abuse. We called the drugs uppers and downers. I knew some other addicts who were experimenting with these same drugs who died.

The way that the Fabian therapists got me out of this destructive habit was to use talk therapy to convince me to quit all drugs and alcohol long enough that they could use EMA therapy with me. Then we focused on happy memories of times when I was not drunk or under the influence of drugs. We did this EMA process repeatedly and intensively. This focus on happy times when I was sober helped me to realize that I could enjoy life without drugs, and that I didn't need to commit suicide by overdosing on them. I never went back to taking dangerous uppers and downers. The EMA therapy probably saved my life. But you won't find that type of life-affirming approach used in drug treatment centers or any other therapeutic institution. Instead they use Illuminati mind control techniques to attack the natural personality of the individual.

Speaking Out

If you have been the victim of trauma-based mind control and you have recovered from it, you may or may not want to speak out in public about what is going on. For myself, I finally realized that it was necessary to my spiritual wellbeing that I find my voice and speak out. In recent years, I have been involved with Thought Crime Radio, which was a radio program on KOPN – and it still has a website (ThoughtCrimeRadio.net). I was a co-host on that radio program for a while where I openly talked about the Illuminati and their mind-control methods. As the result of this, some people who are within the Illuminati, who have become disillusioned with the Illuminati, have contacted me in private and have been feeding me more insider information. Apparently Fabian Therapy for deprogramming Illuminati mind control still exists and is still being secretly used. But it is only being used for the benefit of a small number of people who are wealthy and connected with the Illuminati. So knowledge about this type of therapy is still being suppressed from public knowledge. I've told you here as much about this therapy approach as I feel safe in doing. If you are interested in healing the victims of Illuminati mind control, I hope you are successful.

Right now the Illuminati still seems to be all-powerful. However, I have reason to believe that someday the Illuminati will fall. Although at the present time, the highest-ranking members of the Illuminati all seem unified in their purpose and actions, it is known to many insiders that this cannot last. Right now the Illuminati are continually increasing their wealth and power by systematically looting the middle class. But eventually they will have to turn against each other. This is more than just a hopeful theory, it is a mathematical certainty that the Illuminati will disassemble at some point. This is why the attitude of some Committee members is changing. Every day more and more people outside the Illuminati are becoming aware of it and the harm it does. An opposition movement to deconstruct the Illuminati is growing and it will eventually succeed. However, for most people in America, things will get worse before they get better. During the chaotic times that come, there may be opportunities to help some of the victims of Illuminati mind control.

Perhaps the ideas presented here will be helpful in doing that. I know that there are other people who are aware of Illuminati mind control and are trying to come up with psychological techniques for helping its victims. Someday a standardized approach for dealing with trauma-based mind control victims needs to be developed because of the widespread epidemic that has been going on in our country and the world.

Fabian Therapy for Helping Abductees

I do know that the Fabian therapists did work with some victims who had been abducted by hostile extraterrestrials and that they were known to have gotten positive results. But my Fabian therapists had only just begun to do this type of work when they were killed. However, there can be no doubt that some abductees suffer greatly from the abuse they've received at the hands of their alien abductors.

The most famous abduction is the case of Betty and Barney Hill. After their abduction experience they were aware of missing time, but they were not aware of what happened. They visited a psychiatrist who put them under hypnosis. They recounted almost identical stories, even though they were hypnotized separately. The psychiatrist had them relive the experience over and over again in therapy. Now this did a great deal to publicize the abduction phenomena, but there is nothing to indicate that it helped Betty and Barney Hill to heal emotionally from the experience. In fact, the approach used by the psychiatrist may have made things worse for the Hills. This is because he was forcing them to relive their trauma, but he was doing nothing to heal their memory system. He simply repeated bypassed their damaged memory system by using hypnosis. This is not the optimum approach. And yet this hypnotherapy approach that has the victims re-experience their abductions is being widely popularized and used around the world.

The Fabian approach to deal with this was to avoid making the client directly re-experience the trauma. They would use EMA as described above to analyze only memories of happy experiences which took place during times of sobriety and health. They would teach the clients various methods to process the negative emotions that would come from having been a victim. These would be things like journaling and the use of art to express the experiences. Eventually the client would restore his or her memory system. So hypnosis would not be used to recall the abduction experiences. But the persons would eventually recall the abduction experiences the same way that they can recall any other experience.

When I recall my childhood abuse, even memories that were once repressed, I recall it the same way that I would an ordinary memory from my childhood. I don't need to go through some special mental process to recall the abuse because my memory system has been rehabilitated. And I never was subjected to hypnosis to recall repressed memories.

This is how it would be for an abductee who used Fabian Therapy to heal his or her memory system. Hypnosis has the potential to create confabulation in the mind of the client. Confabulation is the commingling of memory and imagination. But Fabian Therapy doesn't require hypnosis. Fabian Therapy is designed to eliminate confabulation. EMA of happy memories doesn't re-traumatize the person and is designed to eliminate imagination. The structure of the EMA process discourages imagination by encouraging the direct re-experiencing of the memory. Any traumatic experience such as an alien abduction damages the mind's memory recall mechanism. If you try to recall an overwhelmingly painful memory with EMA you will become traumatized again, and this will keep you from healing the memory recall mechanism. But if you use EMA to focus on only happy memories, this will heal the natural mechanism of memory recall. The journaling and other techniques reduce the negative charge contained in the traumatizing abduction memories. Eventually the abductee will be able to recall the abduction memories as he or she would recall any other memory.

I have personally come to believe that Satanic Ritual Abuse, MK Ultra and Monarch mind control are all really forms of alien mind control. Hostile extraterrestrials manipulate the members of these Luciferian secret societies. The Satanists, psychiatrists and CIA operatives who victimize human beings with mind control are themselves being manipulated by hostile extraterrestrials. The alien overlords of this planet have created a culture in which some humans are exploiting their fellow human beings. The extraterrestrial abduction experience is the direct abuse of a human being with trauma-based mind control. They deliberately terrorize the abductees and inflict unnecessary pain because this suppresses memory recall. But the hostile extraterrestrials also are the originators of MK Ultra and other forms of mind control administered by humans. So the ultimate source for this entire culture of mind control is extraterrestrial.

When I was on the radio as a co-host of Thought Crime Radio, I did a number of shows on the subject of UFOs. These shows received the strongest response of any of the shows that we did. We usually had so many people calling in and making comments that we didn't have time to deal with all the people who wanted to respond. Although we had a strong and positive response to such shows, a number of people working at the radio station objected to them. And this played a part in my being driven off the air.

I've done quite a bit of research on the UFO phenomena, and there can be no doubt that UFOs exist. Anybody who is honest and does the research knows that they exist. There are simply too many credible eye witnesses who have come forward having observed such craft. Some might argue that these craft don't come from an extraterrestrial source, but are merely classified, experimental craft built by our government. And some undoubtably are built by the government. But if you do enough research I believe that it becomes clear that some of these craft are not of human design.

And the same thing could be said for the mind-control techniques. It may be human beings who administer Monarch mind control, but it is an alien technology in the same way that UFOs represent an alien technology.

We are being invaded by hostile extraterrestrials. We can't fight back against them with the Sci-Fi weapons like phaser beams or death rays. We can only fight back against them by freeing our minds and helping others to attain mental liberation.

By Kerth Barker

Angelic Defenders & Demonic Abusers
Memoirs of a Satanic Ritual Abuse Survivor

Cannibalism, Blood Drinking
& High-Adept Satanism

Mental Liberation
Deprogramming Satanic Ritual Abuse, MK Ultra,
Monarch & Illuminati Mind Control

Psychic Development
for Prosperity, Self Defense & Political Influence

See http://angelicdefenders.theshamecampaign.com

Made in the USA
Lexington, KY
23 August 2018